JESUS OF NAZARETH

Jesus of Nazareth

by

Josiah C. Russell

PAGEANT PRESS, INC.

TABLE OF CONTENTS

TABLE OF CONTENTS

Preface

Preface

One who presents another account of Jesus of Nazareth and early Christian literature should either offer new evidence or prepare a new interpretation of the evidence, since so many studies consider the career of Christ from many points of view. Still, the result has been, in spite of much agreement upon phases of the evidence, a wide range of interpretations. It is another interpretation that I offer: that before his Mission Jesus had had a successful business career, probably outside of Palestine. That, instead of being a village carpenter, he was, like many other religious leaders, a man of wide experience and probably of considerable wealth.

Since the causes of one's development of theories are often interesting and always instructive, I give mine. For years I had thought of the career of Jesus of Nazareth as a great paradox: the teachings of a village prophet in an agricultural setting became the basis for an urban religion in which non-Christians were called pagans, that is, country dwellers. However, in an article (which I have not been able to find again) the author argued that Jesus must have been a farmer rather than a carpenter. His argument that Jesus was not a carpenter was stronger than his evidence that Jesus was a farmer. This idea eventually led to a study of the evidence and to the conclusion stated above. This explanation would eliminate the paradox: if Jesus spent his early life in the cities near Galilee and there acquired many of his ideas and attitudes, particularly those similar to Epicureanism, his doctrines and points of view might have a natural appeal to the urban Roman culture. And a natural explanation is usually more appealing to a historian than a paradox.

The crux of the question of Jesus' profession before he began his mission centers in two statements about his return to Nazareth. The first, "Is not this the carpenter, the son of Mary and the brother of James and Joses and Judas and Simon and are not his sisters with us?". (Mk. 6:3), provides the conventional interpretation that before his mission Jesus was a carpenter. The second statement, "Doubtless you will quote to me the proverb, 'Physician, heal yourself; what we have heard you did at Capernaum, do here also in your own country'" (Lk. 4:23), might suggest that he was a physician. The first statement would give only what the village folk remembered Jesus to have been when he resided at Nazareth, perhaps as much as twenty years before. The second may be interpreted as a figurative statement, but it could have had a double meaning which would have been peculiarly effective if Jesus had been a physician. The problem then includes the question where he had spent the preceding years, as well as what he had done. Physician or not, he may have been particularly successful in attaining wealth and a knowledge of the world outside of Galilee. The evidence of this is presented as a basis for the hypothesis of his career.

This new interpretation makes the career of Jesus less miraculous and yet more impressively human. For a village carpenter to aspire to a career as a Hebrew prophet and to have a certain success in it is rather difficult, although not impossible, to explain. John the Baptizer, proclaiming a simple return to faith symbolized by baptism, is easy to understand. But the gospel of Christ was more subtle, more far-reaching, more promising for the improvement of the world and the regeneration of mankind. The drama of a man who had had success by the world's standards and yet was willing to surrender it all for the career of a prophet saving the world through the conversion of an agricultural countryside, believing that the leaders of the group would commence a world revolution required to bring heaven to earth, is intense. The tortured remark about the difficulty of a rich man's entering the kingdom of heaven might well be a reminiscence of his struggle to decide whether to continue a career of charity or to make the supreme attempt at religious conversion of Galilee.

If one accepts the conventional interpretation of Jesus' life, he assumes that Jesus spent his life to the time of the mission as a carpenter at Nazareth or in the surrounding area. He would presumably have shared in the local points of view even if blessed by a fine mind and beautiful spirit. The question presented here is whether the mission would have come more naturally from one whose earlier years had been spent outside of Galilee in the Roman and Greek world, one who had shared very successfully in the life of that world and had come to appreciate its values. Indeed, it is a problem to reconcile a career of a village carpenter with no apparent experience in religious leadership with the rather extraordinary career of Jesus of Nazareth. Such questions as these occurred: Why should a village carpenter be meditating upon the temptations which Israel would face when it acquired wealth? Why should Jesus have had so many wealthy friends, even in Jerusalem? Why should he have acquired such a benevolent attitude toward the Romans while living in Zealot country? Why should he have presented the Prodigal Son in such a sympathetic light? In short, how can one set up a consistent career on the basis of all the rather large amount of evidence available?

Of course, one question which arises immediately upon considering this extension and revision of the biography of Jesus of Nazareth is why no one has produced such an hypothesis before. Normally, when one is inclined to disbelieve in the life as set up in conventional terms, he has a tendency to disbelieve most of the life, as do Loisy and Guignebert. On the other hand, if he believes, then it is difficult to produce any but the conventional biography. Many years ago, while studying the lives of the writers of thirteenth-century England, I learned of the almost terrible strength of tradition, particularly if that tradition has been accepted and repeated by men of reputation. It is really difficult for people to comprehend that outstanding scholars are not infallible, at least in matters which do not seem to be controversial. And this reputation for infallibility seems to adhere even more closely to interpretations and conjectures than to matters based upon a solid factual structure. And, of course, much of the data for the life of Christ is subject to a considerable degree of question.

When the interpretations of individual items in a biography are so various, it is the total picture which must be considered. Does the character emerging from the evidence seem to have the proper qualifications and description for him to fit naturally into the historical background and fill the place he took in the environment of that day. Is the Jesus presented here one who might naturally take the place in the religious development of the Roman Empire, and even in his native Palestine, which is required?

Finally, the reader would undoubtedly like to know what bias the writer has or perhaps, less crudely, what is the writer's background. Religiously, the author is a member of the Society of Friends, perhaps of the more cosmopolitan persuasion within it. His background intellectually has been that of a student and professor of history in a number of institutions. His research and publications have ranged from intellectual history to more recent emphasis upon population and its corollaries.

JESUS OF NAZARETH

Nazareth in Galilee

Jesus grew up in Nazareth in Galilee, and thus had a small village in Palestine as the background of his early life. Galilee was the northernmost of the Jewish divisions. On its east is the Lake of Gennesaret, or as it is often called, the Sea of Galilee, which was regarded as within the province. To the west lies a hilly country of great fertility. Of the country, just after this time, a widely traveled and well-educated historian, Josephus, wrote (Bellum Judaicum. iii, 41–43):

> With this limited area, and although surrounded by powerful foreign nations, the two Galilees have always resisted any hostile invasion, for the inhabitants are from infancy inured to war, and have at all times been numerous; never did the men lack courage nor the country men. For the land is everywhere so rich in soil and pasturage and produces such variety of trees that even the most indolent are tempted by these facilities to devote themselves to agriculture.

Josephus himself had led the revolt of one of its cities against the Roman Empire and had held out against none other than Vespasian, probably the ablest general of the Romans, for forty-seven days (Bell. Jud. iii, 110–344).

It is not surprising that Galilee produced as its one local school of political philosophy the most patriotic and vigorous of all the Jewish ideologies, the Zealot. In the time of the Roman procurator Coponius (about A.D. 6–9), "A Galilean, named Judas, incited his countrymen to revolt, upbraiding them as cowards for consenting to pay tribute to the Romans and tolerating mortal masters, after having God for their lord. This man was a sophist who founded a sect of his own, having nothing in common with the others" (Josephus, *Bell. Jud.* ii, 117–118). Yet this is what might be expected of a kind of frontier province with a tradition of vigorous defense of its rights. One might expect also that the provincialism of the area would be strong, particularly in the interior. Certainly one would be surprised if a pacifist sect arose there.

However, Nazareth lies nearly five miles from the great plain of Esdraelon in Samaria, through which the River Kishon flows and along which moved traffic from Phoenicia to the lower Jordan Valley and Jerusalem. Phoenicia was only a dozen or so miles to the east. Nazareth, then, was on the border of a frontier province, the kind of location where influences of all sorts converge. The religious capital was Jerusalem, some seventy miles to the south. The nearest city of some size was the capital of the province, Tiberias, about sixteen miles to the east on the Sea of Galilee. Nazareth had a synagogue and thus was probably a town of a few thousands. From Nazareth Jesus drew many of his illustrations of small-town life and its agricultural environment, which make his teachings so interesting. Nevertheless, Nazareth was an inconsequential town, apparently never mentioned earlier in history. No wonder that Nathaniel quipped, "Can any good thing come out of Nazareth?" (Jn. 2:46). Despite the fact that this remark was good-natured twitting from a resident of nearby Cana (Jn. 21:2), it probably does give a reasonably good estimate of Nazareth.

Even within such a small community, the family of Jesus was not prominent. When, perhaps forty years after Jesus' death, two efforts were made to recover the genealogy of Joseph, the results differed sharply (Mt. 1:15; Lk. 3:23):

Joseph	Joseph
Jacob	Heli
Matthan	Matthat
Eleazar	Levi
Eliud	Melchi
Achim	Jannai

Though few people kept their genealogies as carefully as did the Jews, the result of the research indicates only the most modest position of the family. Joseph was a carpenter, which perhaps meant a builder as well. Virtually nothing else is known of him and not really much more about Mary, despite the exalted position in Christian theology which she was to attain.

Not much information is available about the early years of Christ. The stories told about him are based mostly upon two lines of conjecture. The first is the assumption that, since Jesus was the Redeemer and Savior of Mankind prophesied in the Scriptures of the Jews, prophecies with respect to the career of the Savior must have been fulfilled by Jesus: things such as being the son of David, being born in Bethlehem, and having various experiences considered as necessary to happen to the Savior. The second line was that of the usual attributions to important persons, such as wonderful occurrences at the birth of the person and miracles performed by him in the course of his life. Yet evidence relating to Jesus was so

3

sacred that it was preserved with care, even though it might seem to contradict the prophecies he should fulfill. The running controversy between these lines of biographical influence will be traced in the last two chapters. What might be regarded as historical evidence will be presented now.

From certain statements in the Gospels some indication of the time of the birth of Jesus may be hazarded. He was said to have been about thirty at the beginning of his mission (Lk. 3:23). This presumably means that he was in his thirties, since this was the custom with respect to defining age. It was after the beginning of the public career of John the Baptist, which Luke defines as in the fifteenth year of Tiberius Caesar, and thus from 19 September, 28 to A.D. 29. (Lk. 3:1). However, not much later the Jews are alleged to have said to Jesus, "You are not yet fifty years of age and have you seen Abraham?" (Jn. 8:57). The fifty years were an exaggeration, but it does suggest that Christ was in his late rather than early thirties, and thus would have been born about 5–10 B. C. The introduction to Luke speaks of the birth of Jesus as in the time of Herod, who died in 4 B.C. (Lk.1:5), and then mentions that a decree went out from Caesar Augustus that all the world be enrolled (Lk. 2:1). Augustus did have a census of Roman citizens in 8 B.C. which may properly have been associated with the time of Jesus' birth, although it did not touch those who were not citizens. Jewish opinion was so hostile to censuses (II Sam. 2:1–16) that suggestion of an association with a census would have been most unpropitious if it had not been true. The identification of the census with that of Quirinus of 7 A.D. was thus a bad guess being much too late.

That Jesus was born in Galilee seems probable from

4

the statement that his native city was in that area (Mk. 6:1). Since he was called Jesus of Nazareth, that city has a claim as his birthplace. An objection to this assumption is that to be called "of Nazareth" was a Greek rather than a Jewish form of designation. If, as I believe, he spent much time among the Greeks, there is no objection on this point. The usual attribution of his birth to Bethlehem is assumed to be the result of the Scriptural prediction that he would be born in David's city (Mt. 2:5; Lk. 2:4).

This raises the question as to whether the first two chapters of Matthew and Luke contain anything credible. The circumstances of the creation of these chapters will be given in the study of the development of Christian literature in the first century. One point of view is that given above, that only a few items may be believed, while the opposite point of view is of wholesale acceptance. In between there are many positions. A quite conjectural story of the first years of Christ's life may be derived in the following way. It assumes that the expression "But Mary kept all these things, pondering them in her heart" (Lk. 2:19) may actually represent a small fund of information much changed by both Mary's pondering and the legend-izing which went on in the first century. The crucifixion and early years of Christianity doubtless changed Mary's ideas about points which she recollected, and early Christians also saw different significance in them, as well as embellishing the story with ornaments suitable for the life of a great religious leader.

The key to the evidence would appear to be the story of the birth in a stable. Its credibility comes from the fact that it was not required by Scripture for the Messiah and that the association with the House of David would normally demand a more exalted birthplace. The manger in the stable also assumes birth on a journey. The place need not have been far away from Nazareth. If the indication that his birthplace was in or near Galilee is correct, it might have been some place like Bethshean (Scythopolis), just across the border in Gilead on the highway to Jerusalem. Some such name, especially if it began with Beth, would be easy to alter to Bethlehem, to have him born in the right city.

If we assume that Jesus was born in a stable, certain other easy assumptions follow. The shepherds (Lk. 2:8–20) might have dropped in to talk with the family. The star (Mt. 2:2,9) could have been almost any very bright star, a subject of conversation. The very unusual conjunctions of Jupiter and Saturn occurred three times in 7 B.C., not long after the Roman census of 8 B.C. Travelers in the inn, perhaps even from far places, might have given gifts to the child and spoken to the parents about the census (Mt. 2:1–12). In short, memories of rather simple acts may have been the starting point of the later legends, even in Mary's mind.

A second key to the evidence seems to be association with Jerusalem and the Temple. A relative, Zechariah, was a priest there (Lk. 1:8–9), and Mary had gone to visit his wife not long before the journey (Lk. 1:39). The visit for the purification was routine (Lk. 2:22–24), but the detail about the hopes and lives of Simeon (Lk. 2:25–35) and Anna (Lk. 36–38) are not. It would seem, unless we assume that these two were divinely drawn to the family at the time of the sacrifice, that Joseph and Mary were well acquainted with them and so knew their hopes and lives intimately. Only later did Mary and others relate these hopes to Jesus. This association with the Temple thus would seem of some length. It suggests that possibly Joseph was engaged in some of the construction going on about the Temple in those days, even though

6

the main part seems to have been completed some years earlier. After all, he was a carpenter.

This would imply that the family stayed in Jerusalem some time. Such a stay is assumed in the story of the flight to Egypt (Mt. 2:13–18), since they were said to have returned only on the death of Herod, in 4 B.C. The story of Herod's slaughter of the innocents doubtless comes from his killing of three of his sons in 6–4 B.C. and the rounding up of the Jewish leaders with orders to kill them at his death, orders fortunately not carried out. The reason for returning to Nazareth, it might he hazarded, was that Joseph's employment ceased on Herod's death. Again the nucleus of these stories might have been the memory of Mary or others in the family.

If this reconstruction is accurate, it would place Joseph's family in a somewhat different position from that of a simple carpenter's family in a remote Galilean village. Years in Jerusalem should have given it a place in that city, since it was probably not over ten or, at most, twenty thousand persons in size. The yearly return at the Passover (Lk. 2:41) would have renewed such acquaintances and have provided a base for later activities of Jesus. As a village carpenter Jesus could hardly have evoked the respect and devotion that were manifested at the end of his life by such outstanding men as Joseph of Arimathea and Nicodemus. It is difficult to believe that such devotion could have been accomplished by a Mission of about a year, most of which was spent outside of Jerusalem.

If Joseph did work in the Temple area, another explanation of the incident of Jesus as a twelve-year-old (Lk. 2:41–51) is possible. Normally a boy was bar mitzvahed in his thirteenth year, after a certain amount of instruction—that Jesus in his twelfth year showed such interest was thus a sign of great precocity. His answer,

"Did you not know that I must be in my father's house?" might have referred to that fact that Joseph had worked there. Many children have a possessive attitude toward places of family employment. Here again, Mary may have remembered what at the time seemed merely a bright saying, but was to be invested with religious significance at a later date.

The relationship of Jesus to the several persons called his brothers and sisters in the Gospels has been a matter of controversy primarily because the doctrine of the Virgin Birth made it very necessary to deny that they were his full brothers and sisters. The chief evidence about the family is a statement in Mark (6:3) alleged by persons at Nazareth when He preached there first: "And on the sabbath he began to teach in the synagogue and many who heard him were astonished, saying, 'Where did this man get all this?—Is this not the carpenter, the son of Mary and brother of James and Joses and Judas and Simon, and are not his sisters with us?' Luke has (4:16,22) "And he came to Nazareth where he had been brought up —Is not this Joseph's son?" Matthew gives (13:53): "Is not this the carpenter's son? Is not his mother called Mary? And are not his brothers James and Joseph and Simon and Judas? And are not all his sisters with us?" From these items, as well as from the circumstance that Nathaniel, who came from Cana (Jn. 21:2) and was probably a resident of Capernaum, since he was a friend of Philip (Jn. 1:44), yet did not know Jesus, a very tentative outline of the family history can be constructed.

Only the sisters were still at Nazareth, presumably because they were married or employed there. In either case the family had probably lived in that village until the sisters were grown. At the time of the Mission, Mary was apparently living at Cana (Jn. 2:1), presumably with one of the sons. Since Nathaniel, who was of Cana, did not

8

know Jesus at the time that he became a disciple, Jesus had probably never lived at Cana. In a small town like Cana a resident would have heard of newcomers even if he had left the village himself. Indeed, Nathaniel would have known Jesus if Jesus had lived in the Capernaum-Bethsaida area recently. As we shall see, the easiest explanation of the ready answer to Jesus' call by several of his disciples was that Jesus had himself lived in the area for a time, and thus appealed to persons with whom he was well acquainted.

In appearance Jesus was a small and rather unimpressive man. Many years ago conclusive evidence was presented for the smallness of Jesus' stature, a height of about five feet, two inches.[1] It was shown, for instance, that Luke's words in the well-known incident of Zacchaeus climbing a tree could as readily mean that Christ was small as that the climber was (Lk. 19:1–10). Thus illustrations of how great things might come from small sources may have been designed to suggest that great ideas and thoughts might come from one as small as Jesus. The addition of a cubit to Jesus' height might have made a difference to him.

Under these circumstances it is not surprising that Jesus' relations with his family were not close at the beginning of his mission. In fact, at that time it seems to have disapproved of his mission and may even have doubted his sanity (Mk. 3:31–35; Lk. 8:19–21; Mt. 12:46–50). On the occasion of the appearance of his family, asking to see him, he said, "Who is my family?" Only after his death did his family become prominent members of the Christian group. His brother, James, was head of the Jerusalem community for many years before he was martyred. Jesus, then, may have left the family perhaps as long as twenty years before the mission.

That he was a carpenter until he was in his thirties

seems ruled out by two lines of reasoning. The first is that a long period of practicing this trade should have resulted in a considerable number of relics which would have become very precious in the years following the crucifixion. None seems to have remained.[2] The second is that of the many sayings of Jesus, hardly one shows the remotest interest in carpentry and little in building. This is the more astonishing since he talked of many phases of village life: the oven, the children's games, the patched clothes, the lost penny, and village marriage, as well as of the crops in the fields. The carpenter shop is so conspicuously absent that even a dislike for it may be surmised.

If the carpenter shop in the village was not attractive, the cities nearby may have been, as they have been to so many intelligent young men of all times. Ancient cities, like modern ones, had too few children to replace the adults, so the deficit was filled by migration from the countryside. From Nazareth, Ptolemais (Acre), a modest seaport, was only twenty miles. To the north of Nazareth the great ports of Tyre and Sidon lay twenty five and forty-five miles, respectively. Along the coast to the southwest was Caesarea, a considerable port and Roman administrative center for Samaria and Judea, about twenty-seven miles from Nazareth as the crow flies. Damascus was seventy miles to the east. The nearest Galilean city, as mentioned above, was Tiberias, but the Capernaum-Bethsaida area, where Jesus spent much of his mission, was some miles north of Tiberias. Probably Jesus went there at some time early in his life, and made the acquaintance of many of the families from which he later drew his followers. But his appeal to them would have been greater if it followed a notably successful career in the larger world outside of Galilee.

II

Early Manhood

That Jesus was interested in travelers and traveling is clear from his stories. The Good Samaritan places help to a traveler upon a high plane of interest (Lk. 10:29–37). Jesus seems to speak from the point of view of one who appreciated the problem of travel in an age of poor police protection. In the parable of the Prodigal Son, the plight of the prodigal who has succumbed to the temptations of the city is told with surprising sympathy (Lk. 15:11–32). The villain of the story is actually the older brother, who viewed the return with somewhat less than enthusiasm. Indeed, it is hard to imagine a lifelong resident of Nazareth telling such stories, especially to other Galileans. Besides these stories as evidence of interest in travel, there is the record of almost continuous travel about Galilee, Samaria, and Judea in the rather short mission. In marked contrast, John the Baptist seems to have selected a favorable spot on the Jordan where he might baptize and preach to the people coming to him there.

Jesus may have spent at least a part of his early life in the area about Capernaum-Bethsaida-Chorazin, and thus had friends and acquaintances there. From that area he drew many of his disciples, some of whom he probably knew earlier than his mission. Indeed, it is difficult to believe that he could say to Andrew, Peter,

James, John, and Philip, "Come with me," unless he had had previous acquaintance with them which provided some evidence of his power. This alone would make it hard to understand how a village carpenter of no special distinction could command the instant response that both the Synoptics and John allege, although they differ as to the place of the call. And one would have expected Jesus to have visited Jerusalem regularly as a religious man over the years before the mission, visits which could have secured the friendship of Jewish leaders. Again, the calibre of men like Nicodemus and Joseph of Arimathea suggests a person of considerable stature intellectually and perhaps financially.

The name "Jesus of Nazareth" is a gentile form: its use suggests extra-Jewish relations during his life. There is a specific reference to a visit outside of Galilee, "He went to the region of Tyre and Sidon" (Mk. 7:24–30), partially suppressed by Matthew (15:21–28). There, although he would not have anyone know of his presence, a Greek woman, Syro-Phoenician by race, immediately importuned him to help her daughter. The implication would seem to be that she had known him from previous residence there. "If the mighty works done in you had been done in Tyre and Sidon, they would have repented long ago" also suggests knowledge of those cities (Lk. 10:13–15; Mt. 11:20–22). And when Jesus said that he was leaving Jerusalem, "The Jews said to one another, 'Where does this man intend to go that we shall not find him? Does he intend to go to the Dispersion among the Greeks and teach the Greeks?'" (Jn. 7:35). The Dispersion was the series of scattered Jewish settlements: the nearest were probably in Caesarea, Tyre, and Sidon. And the statement strongly suggests that Jesus knew Greek.

Luke's account of the incident at Nazareth would

have had more point if Jesus had been living abroad in the region of Tyre and Sidon (Lk. 4:23–28):

> But in truth, I tell you, there were many widows in Israel in the days of Elijah, when the heaven was shut up three years and six months, when there came a great famine over all the land; and Elijah was sent to none of them but only to Zarepheth, in the land of Sidon, to a woman who was a widow. And there were many lepers in Israel in the time of the prophet Elisha; and none of them was cleansed, but only Naamon the Syrian.

It suggests that Christ had been asked why anyone who had been living abroad could bring a message to them such as he was bringing.

Traditions asserted also that Jesus had been to Egypt in his early manhood and had studied magic there.[1] This is rather interesting if very conjectural, since several persons from the area of Egypt and Cyrene were prominent in early Christian circles. And magic was apt to be associated with medicine.

The story of the Syro-Phoenician woman summoning Jesus to care for her daughter (Mk. 7:26–30) rather suggests that Jesus was a physician. Of course his long record of healing is regarded as the result of religious power rather than of medical knowledge. However, no such long and elaborate education was necessary to qualify a man for a medical career as is required today. Apparently one got his training directly from another doctor, usually by going with the doctor as he visited his patients. The Pharisees and others apparently never questioned Jesus' ability to heal, somewhat easier to understand if he had a reputation as a physician before coming to Galilee than if he had been merely a village carpenter. And there is the version of his meeting at Nazareth (Lk. 4:3):

> And he said to them, "Doubtless you will quote me this proverb, 'Physician, heal yourself'; what we have heard you did at Capernaum, do here also in your country!"

Usually "physician" is assumed to be used here in a non-literal sense. However, the ancient-medieval world was a visual-minded world, and it is always well to consider the possibility that an author meant exactly what he said. And if Jesus was ill at the time, as is possible, the statement would have had even more point.

A second possibility is that he may have been a merchant of pearls. He held a very high opinion of these jewels (Mt. 7:6):

> Do not give dogs what is holy; and do not throw your pearls before swine, lest they trample them underfoot and turn to attack you.

In the series of statements which included the parables of the mustard seed and the leaven there is the following (Mt. 13:45—46):

> Again, the kingdom of heaven is like a merchant in search of fine pearls, who, on finding one pearl of great value, went and sold all that he had and bought it.

If Christ regarded pearls as "holy," the sale of his pearls to attain the kingdom of heaven would be merely substituting a higher holiness for a lesser. One might notice also that pearls were essentially a marine product, normally handled by fishermen and sailors as well as by

14

merchants. Christ's interest in water and waterfolk was remarkable. Not only was he about the Sea of Galilee a good deal, but he chose several disciples from among its fishermen. If one would conjecture wildly, he might suggest that Jesus made money as a merchant which enabled him to pay for an apprenticeship in medicine.

There is evidence that Christ did very well financially. Let us look at 1 Corinthians 8:1–5.

> We want you to know, brethren, about the grace of God which has been shown in the churches of Macedonia, for in a severe test of affliction, their abundance of joy and their extreme poverty have overflowed in a wealth of liberality on their part. For they gave according to their means, as I can testify, and beyond their means of their own free will, begging us earnestly for the favor of taking part in the relief of the saints—and this, not as we expected, but first they gave themselves and to us by the will of God.

The rest is a request for continuing the giving. The whole chapter, indeed, is devoted to finances: It is a letter to what was the wealthiest and probably the largest among the Greek cities, a city famous for its luxury and an immorality which tainted even the Christians there (1 Cor., 5). This section is usually regarded as furnishing the best texts for appeals to "Christian stewardship."

The chapter continues (8:8–11):

> I say this is not a command, but to prove by the earnestness of others that your love also is genuine. For you know the grace of our Lord Jesus Christ, that *though he was rich*, yet for

your sake *he became poor,* so that by his poverty you might become rich. And in this matter I give my advice: it is best for you now to complete what a year ago you began not only to do but to desire, so that your readiness in desiring it may be matched by your completing it out of what you have. (Italics added.)

What was Christ rich in which he gave up and in which he became poor? The grace of God of verse 1 was evidently in money—the parallel here (grace of our Lord) would seem to demand the same. If one says that he was rich in divinity, one can hardly say that he lost it, even to give religion to his followers, in which obviously they became rich. If life alone is meant, he could have said it easily, but he is obviously talking about money. It is worth considering, then, the hypothesis that Paul meant exactly what he said, that Christ was wealthy.

Presumably St. Paul meant that Jesus spent his wealth in the course of his ministry. Is there evidence of this?

Just before the feeding of the five thousand, the disciples asked Jesus (Mk. 6:37), "Shall we go and buy two hundred denarii worth of bread and give it to them to eat?" That amount was a large sum of money, as one might surmise from the fact that it was expected to buy bread for five thousand people. Yet there is no hint that they did not have it. The problem of money never seems to arise. Zebedee, the father of James and John, had hired servants (Mk. 1:20), which implies some affluence. And some women "provided for them out of their means" (Lk. 8:1–3), but this may mean little more than that they provided food for the group. Jesus is never accused of living off his followers, an easy accusation for critics to have made even if it were only partially true. And if

16

Jesus was wealthy, it explains why Judas may have found it attractive to have been his treasurer (Jn. 13:29).

One might doubt, of course, that Jesus was wealthy because of his strong statement about the difficulty of a man of wealth in attaining heaven. Yet he was apparently not hostile to acquiring wealth. Take, for instance, the story of the talents or the pounds (Mt. 5:14–30; Lk. 19:12–26). In the version of Matthew a man gave his servants money to use while he was away.

> And he who had received the five talents came forward, bringing five talents more, saying "Master, you delivered to me five talents; here I have made five talents more." His master said to him, "Well done, good and faithful servant; you have been faithful over a little, I will set you over much; enter into the joy of your master." (The servant who received one talent had hid his money in the ground.) "You wicked and slothful servant! ... You ought to have invested my money with the bankers, and at my coming I should have received what was my own with interest."

Now the talent was a very large sum of money. Here is approval, even a kind of sophisticated approval of what might be regarded as high finance. Jesus obviously did not disapprove of making money from interest. His approval of business appears elsewhere, as, for instance, when he adjured his followers not to swear at all, (Mt. 5:33–37), a practice usually accompanying bargaining in business practice at that time. If Jesus had gained wealth in spite of not participating in such practices, he would have spoken with great authority to those who knew of it.

17

If Jesus was a man of wealth, the story of the marriage feast at Cana might be interpreted differently from the standard treatment: that the wine had run out and was replaced by a miracle of Jesus, the first of his Mission. The conversation is said to have run as follows: (Jn. 2:1–11):

Mary. They have no wine.
Jesus. O woman what have you to do with me? My hour is not yet come.
Mary (*to servants*). Do whatever he tells you.
Jesus (*to servants*). Fill the jars with water. Now draw some and take it to the feast.
Steward (*to bridegroom*). Every man serves the good wine first; and when men have drunk freely, then the poor wine; but you have kept the good wine until now.

The answer of Jesus to Mary is incomprehensible to us as it stands, but it evidently meant something to Mary, who immediately gave the order to the servants. Was it a signal from Jesus to Mary? That, instead of water, the bags held good wine brought by Jesus. The episode then ended hilariously for Jesus and Mary, if it brought some confusion to the bridegroom. The incident reads like one of Mary's happier memories, comparable to the story of Jesus in the Temple. It tends to show a close feeling between Mary and Jesus. Taken too seriously by others, it was converted into the first miracle of the mission. Obviously the relation of Jesus and his family had changed by the beginning of the Mission from the happy association indicated at Cana.

Furthermore, Jesus seemed very much at ease with wealthy men, even with those tax gatherers so generally disliked in Palestine. Zacchaeus, the rich publican, who

18

had climbed the tree to see Jesus, was asked to entertain him (Lk. 19:1–10). Matthew, or Levi, another tax gatherer, after being invited to become a disciple, gave a great banquet for Jesus and his followers (Mk. 2:13–17; Mt. 9:9–13; Lk. 5:27–32). This association with publicans and sinners was very distasteful to the Jewish leaders (Lk. 15:1–2). Yet Jesus was also associated with outstanding Pharisees and other Jewish leaders of a more conventional type. Nicodemus, a leader of Jerusalem, went to him by night (Jn. 3:1–15), tried to secure justice for Jesus (Jn. 7:50–52), and brought spices for Jesus' burial (Jn. 19:39). Another leader, Joseph of Arimathea, received Christ's body for burial after the crucifixion (Mk. 15:42–46; Lk. 23:50–53; Jn. 19:38–41), and in one version is called a rich man. The nature of Christ's association with these men is not certain, of course, but one may suspect that their associations antedated the mission, especially if Jesus had been a wealthy man in that period. Indeed, the mystery of Judas is easier to understand if we assume that he was an earlier business associate of Jesus who continued as his treasurer but either disliked or never understood Jesus' mission.

Outside of Galilee he would have been more likely to acquire a different and more tolerant attitude toward the Roman Empire than either at Jerusalem or at home. Galilee, as mentioned earlier, was a center famous for its hostility to the Empire. The Pharisees tested him by asking, in the well-known incident (Mk. 12:14; Mt. 22:17) "Is it lawful to pay taxes to Caesar, or not?" "Render unto Caesar the things that are Caesar's, and to God the things that are God's" showed a willingness to accept Caesar as head of government. The same spirit appears in the payment of the half shekel at Capernaum (Mt. 17:24). His compliment to the centurion (Mt. 8:5; Lk. 7:2–10) indicates his appreciation of the civil function of the man. His prophecy about the destruction of Jerusalem, (Mt. 24:1–2; Lk. 21:20–24), if not a comment of the evangelist after the loss of the city, might have come from his knowledge of the small size of Jerusalem compared with the great size of other cities. The attitude of Jesus was more that of a rich and tolerant citizen of the Empire than of a carpenter in a village like Nazareth. Had he even been a Jewish resident in the poorer quarter of a Roman city, he might have retained the provincial outlook.

The Jews outside of Palestine had a very different attitude from those within the Empire. The Empire, particularly under Augustus and Claudius, protected the Jews in their peculiar beliefs.[2] This protection naturally gave the Jews a feeling of gratitude toward the Empire but not toward the other religions of the area. In this respect a distinction should probably be made between the situation in the great city of Alexandria and the rest of the Empire. In the city there was a very large colony of Jews, perhaps a fifth of the area's population. Confident because of their numbers, the Jewish group there seems to have adopted a superior and intolerant attitude toward the pagan religions, thus arousing their intense dislike. Sharp encounters broke out between them. The better information about Jews in Alexandria may have given a wrong impression that their attitudes and encounters were typical of the whole Empire. This seems very unlikely to have been true of smaller centers, where the Jews were intermingled with the local population and generally shared their points of view. This would be especially true of the wealthier Jews, who would tend to associate with other people of wealth on a social rather than a racial basis.

The evidence, then, about Jesus' life before the Mission is heavily conjectural. If the tradition had been in favor of a life in the cities of Syria, everything known about his ideas and life would have fitted nicely into it. As it is, the life as a carpenter of Nazareth or in nearby villages does not seem to offer the necessary education or experience required by his career in the Mission. Indeed, it would be very difficult to understand how he would have picked up so many of the characteristics of the Hellenic civilization and of Jewish groups beyond Galilee if he had spent his early manhood in that province. His very inability to convert the masses of Galilee would indicate an essential difference in point of view. His disciples came from the most urban and probably the most sophisticated town of Galilee, that is, Capernaum (and probably the newly built Tiberias). Had he been living in the area over the years, it is unlikely that he would have even tried to convert the villagers, because he would have understood the difficulty of doing it.

III

Early Intellectual Outreach

During the period before the Mission, Jesus' life in the Hellenistic world, if that was where he went, should have broadened his intellectual outlook beyond that which he held in Galilee or even in Jerusalem. One phase of that life would obviously be among the Jews associated with the synagogues of the Dispersion. These should have had members who had Greek interests as well as Hebrew. Jesus' knowledge of the Bible is revealed in his quotations from the Scriptures. He would almost certainly be drawn to explore the religious and intellectual life of the people in the cities, a quest which might have had considerable impact upon his thinking. In that very period much interaction occurred between the Jews and the religions and philosophies of the Empire. It was the period of the great Jewish thinker, Philo of Alexandria, a man whose influence went far beyond his racial group. Indeed, a great empire dominated by a single, all-powerful ruler provided an ideal setting for the spread of the belief in one omnipotent god. The syncretism of the time, which tended to identify gods with similar attributes, was a vital factor in religion then.

Jesus liked to quote certain books of the Old Testament. His favorites, as is clear from quotations in Mark, John, and the matter common to Luke and Matthew (usually called Q), were the Pentateuch, especially Deuteronomy, the Psalms, Daniel, and Isaiah. He shared the common Jewish love of Psalms. From the Pentateuch came many verses dealing with the Law and the early life of the Jews. These include some of the verses upon which he was alleged to have meditated during the Temptation. Daniel was deeply concerned with the relations of the prophet to the administrators and temporal rulers, Nebuchadnezzar and Belshazzar of Babylon and Darius and Cyrus of the Persians. The attraction of Isaiah was that of a great social reformer, although the material in that book is varied and doubtless comes from more than one author. Numerous single quotations from other books than these show a wide acquaintance with Jewish history and the Scriptures. One might suspect that he had in his possession the books most commonly cited.

There is much in Isaiah which would appeal to a Jew outside of Palestine and to a man of deep sympathies, for it is a book widely international in its range. Assyria, Babylon, Philistia, Moab, Damascus, Ethiopia, Egypt, Edom, Arabia all appear in it. Israel's perverseness is castigated, but her relationship to Jehovah offers hope for the future. There is the vision of Jehovah's servant (42:1–7):

> Behold, my servant, whom I uphold; my chosen in whom my soul delighteth; I have put my Spirit upon him; he will bring forth Justice to the Gentiles. He will not cry, nor lift up his voice, nor cause it to be heard in the street. A bruised reed will he not break, and a dimly burning wick will he not quench: he will bring forth justice in truth. He will not fail nor be discouraged, till he set justice in the earth, and the

isles shall wait for his law ... I, Jehovah, have called thee in righteousness, and will hold thy hand, and will keep thee, and give thee for a covenant of the people, for a light of the Gentiles, to open the blind eyes, to bring the prisoners from the dungeon, and them that sit in darkness out of the prison-house.

He is obviously a messenger to the Gentiles as well as to the Jews:

Also the foreigners that join themselves to Jehovah, to minister unto him, and to love the name of Jehovah, to be his servants, every one that keepeth the sabbath from profaning it, and holdeth fast my covenant; even them will I bring to my holy mountain (56:6–7).

"But now, O Jehovah, thou art our Father" (64:8). "And a Redeemer will come to Zion, and unto to them that turn from transgression in Jacob, sayeth Jehovah" (59:20). And what does Jehovah want (1:11–17):

What unto me is the multitude of your sacrifices? saith Jehovah: I have had enough of the burnt offerings of rams, and the fat of fed beasts and I delight not in the blood of bullocks, or of lambs, or of he-goats. When you come to appear before me, who hath required this at your hands, to trample my courts. Bring no more vain oblations; incense is an abomination to me; new moon and sabbath—I cannot away with iniquity and solemn meeting ... Wash you, make you clean; put away the evil of your doing from before mine eyes; cease to do evil; learn to do well; seek justice; relieve the oppressed; judge the fatherless, plead for the widow.

Come now and let us reason together, saith Jehovah: though your sins be as scarlet, they shall be as white as snow; though they shall be red like crimson, they shall be as wool. If ye be willing and obedient, ye shall eat the good of the land: if ye refuse and rebel, ye shall be devoured with the sword; for the mouth of Jehovah hath spoken it.

Jesus seems to have had no special training in the law of the Jews (Jn. 7:5), although he obviously had a considerable knowledge of the Scriptures, such as one would receive from association with any outstanding synagogue. At Nazareth he is said to have read and commented upon Scripture as he was wont to do. He has been suspected of being an Essene during his unknown years.[1] Doubtless, he shared in some of their religious ideas: these were of the common stock of religious thinking in his day. But his attitudes toward women and toward ritual, to name two points of difference, are sufficiently distant from the ideal Essene philosophy to prevent one from believing more than that he was acquainted with and approved of some of their doctrines. The Essenes had a rather rigid approach to life and probably did not have the sense of humor exhibited by Jesus.[2]

Knowing that Christ was interested in apocalyptic books, one might easily admit that he was capable of such sayings as appear in chapter 13 of Mark, especially under the influence of the repressed insurrection and high feeling at Jerusalem. In contrast with the exciting character of such literature were the rather placid, or at least restrained, doctrines of the Epicureans, which were widespread in that day. Yet in many respects their ideas were close to those of the Christians and to the ideas of Christ himself. As a recent writer upon the Christian approval of Epicureanism has stated:

"In summary, we have observed that about the only important Epicurean tenet which does not gain some sort of approval among the Fathers is the denial of divine providence. Almost every other facet of Epicurus' teachings was adopted or adapted by one Father or another."[3] One might almost gather from the quotation that somehow Epicurus intervened in time between Christ and the Fathers with views which were accepted by the Fathers. Let us quote again from an authority on Epicureanism: "His (Epicurus') was the only creed that attained to the dimensions of a world philosophy. For the space of more than seven centuries, three before Christ and four afterward, it continued to command the devotion of men. It flourished among Greeks and barbarians alike, in Greece, Asia Minor, Syria, Judaea, Egypt, Italy, Roman Africa and Gaul. The man himself was revered as an ethical father, a savior, and a god. Men wore his image on fingerrings; they displayed painted portraits of him in their living rooms; the more affluent honored him with likenesses in marble. His handbooks of doctrine were carried about like breviaries; his sayings were esteemed as if oracles and committed to memory as if Articles of Faith. His published letters were cherished as if epistles of an apostle. Pledges were taken to live obedient to his precepts. On the twentieth day of every month his followers assembled to perform solemn rites in honor of his memory, a sort of sacrement."[4]

Such a successful philosophy naturally had enemies. To continue: "Throughout these same seven centuries no man was more ceaselessly reviled. At his first appearance as a public teacher he was threatened with the fate of Socrates. In Athens he never dared to offer instruction in a public place but confined himself to his own house and garden. His character and his doctrines became the special target of abuse for each successive school and sect, first for Platonists, next for Stoics, and finally for Christians. His name became an abomination to orthodox Jews. The Christians, by no means blind to the merits of his ethics, abhorred him for his denial of divine providence and immortality."[5] The differences between Epicureanism and Christianity were sufficient to blind scholars to the possibility that Christ might have been influenced by them. Even the possibility of much contact seems out of range of actuality to a resident of Nazareth. But if Jesus did spend many years in the larger cities of the eastern Mediterranean as a man of some wealth, he must inevitably have been drawn into some contacts with Epicureanism.

The problem of the possible influence of Epicureanism lies in differences from Judaism in view and emphases. One may first point out as evident the lack of influence of Stoicism, which set up personal standards as ideals: temperance, courage, wisdom, and justice. These are qualities which are essentially personal: one could exhibit all of these and be only distantly acquainted with the rest of mankind. In a sense this was also true of Judaism. Take the Ten Commandments. The first four (Jehovah alone, no graven images, no blasphemy, respect for the Sabbath) concern divine-human relationship. Another five forbid certain sins (murder, adultery, theft, false witness, covetousness) and, like Stoic virtues, assume no close positive relationship with the human race. The fifth Commandment, honor of father and mother, does set up a personal relationship.

27

Judaism, furthermore, set up a series of sacrifices, rites, and ceremonies honoring God and drawing the Jews together as a group. Within the group there was expected to be a common association, but the fratricidal struggle within Jerusalem while it was being besieged by the Romans in A.D. 68–70 shows the system's shortcomings. This statement does not do justice to principles worked out by the great teachers of Judaism at the time, such as "Do not unto others what you would not have done unto you." But even this is rather negative, and hardly prescribes pleasant personal relationships as a basis for society.

Epicureanism, on the contrary, presents a series of interpersonal relationships. De Witt's list of Epicurean virtues is honesty, faith, *love of mankind, friendship, suavity,* hope, attention to the present, and *gratitude.*[6] The italicized items are largely interpersonal and the whole program, based on the importance of happiness and pleasure as fundamental ideals, is an endeavor to secure pleasant and wholesome relationships. Indeed, the most distinctive Epicurean characteristic, *suavitas,* involved "a certain agreeableness of speech and manners." Since these ideals were difficult in a world based on a struggle to get ahead, ambition for wealth and power was discouraged. The ideal of nature or admitting and satisfying natural desires was held up, while the dangers of overindulgence or even of human relationships dependent upon them were declared objectionable. Epicureanism was grossly maligned as a philosophy of indulgence of things regarded as wicked by the Greek and as sinful by the Jews and, later, by the Christians. It was the kind of misrepresentation which Jesus pointed out about himself (Lk. 7:34–35): "The Son of man has come eating and drinking; and you say, 'Behold, a glutton and a drunkard, a friend of tax gatherers and sinners.' Yet wisdom is justified by all her children." Epicurus could have said that. The wisdom of Epicurus was not a philosophy for rulers of state or for an exclusive, intolerant religion.

The anti-Epicurean attitude of the early Christian communities was so strong that it may have caused some of Christ's own words to have disappeared. For instance, how did Jesus address the disciples? The associates and later disciples of Epicurus were called Friends of Epicurus.[7] It is possible that Jesus called his disciples "Friends." In Luke (12:4–7) his words are said to have been, "I tell you, my friends, do not fear." These words, as well as other uses of the word "friends" (11:5–8; 14:12; 15:8–9) all seem to come from the document known as L, into which Mark and the common Matthew-Luke material (Q) are fitted. And these seem to be the only instances, outside of casual items (Mk. 3:21; Jn. 15:15) in which the word is used in the Gospels or in St. Paul. And only one instance occurs in Acts (4:23). Probably Jesus did speak of his associates as friends, thus doing both what was natural and what was characteristic of the Epicureans.

Even Epicurus' religious philosophy might have points of appeal. He believed that the gods dwelled on Mt. Olympus, happy and perfect. One should participate in religious rites in their honor, sharing thereby in their happiness and to some extent in their perfection. The gods were friendly, even loving. Epicurus might have written, "on earth as it is in heaven." He believed that the gods did not concern themselves with the affairs of men and thus that they should not be feared. Furthermore, one need not fear death: it was but a dissolution. There are sharp differences between what Epicurus taught and Jesus' point of view, but there might be possibilities of reconciliation.

The study summarized in the quotation about Epicureanism shows how many of the precepts of that philosophy were close to the teachings of Jesus. Jesus' problem, if he appealed to the Jews alone, was to add the happy, personal relationship to their belief in Jehovah and in the Law (with some de-emphasis of details of the latter). In a sense he would emphasize the positive qualities of life to a people whose religion preferred to forbid the negative. The influence then would be to direct their attention to the possibilities opened by the Epicurean approach to life. For an Epicurean to accept Jesus' beliefs, he would have to adjust to the idea of a more personal God and immortality. There would also be the question of the attitude toward the emperor on the part of the Christians unless they were granted the tolerance enjoyed by the Jews in the Empire.

The evidence of the ministry of Jesus shows him a skillful, accomplished teacher, able to hold the attention of large crowds, to evoke the personal loyalty of men and women of different types, and to debate successfully with well-trained religious leaders of the day. That he should suddenly acquire this ability well along in his life would seem a rather unreasonable assumption. The alternative is that he had already developed this ability as a teacher and a prophet before he commenced his ministry in Palestine. When talking of himself as the good shepherd, Jesus is alleged to have said (Jn. 10:16), "And I have other sheep that are not of this fold; I must bring them also, and they will heed my voice. So there shall be one flock, one shepherd." Or those Greeks who wanted to see Jesus (Jn. 12:20–21), where had they heard of Jesus? An even more interesting case is that of the well-known Apollos. In writing to the Corinthians (I, 1:12; 3:22), Paul notes that reports reach him that Christians there are saying: "I belong to Paul, or I belong to Apollos or I belong to Cephas," and the second time they are mentioned: Paul, Apollos, Cephas. The order was presumably that of rank in the Christian movement, perhaps in Corinth. But even there, in one of the great centers of the early missionary effort, it is hard to imagine a leader rated above St. Peter who had not in some way been associated with Jesus.

Knowledge of Apollos' career in Christian ministry come from Acts (18:24–27): "Now, a Jew named Apollos, a native of Alexandria, came to Ephesus. He was an eloquent man, well versed in the scriptures. He had been instructed in the way of the Lord; and being fervent in spirit, he spoke and taught accurately the things concerning Jesus, though he knew only the baptism of John. He began to speak boldly in the synagogue; but when Priscilla and Aquila heard him, they took him and expounded to him the way of God more accurately."

"He knew only the baptism of John" may mean, as it is usually interpreted, that Apollos had been baptized by John and was one of his disciples. But if it means this, how could he have "taught accurately the things concerning Jesus," unless he had met Jesus earlier? And what could Priscilla and Aquila have added, unless it was the story of the Resurrection and of Christ's ministry in Palestine? Apollos was regarded highly, not only as one of the three spiritual sources of inspiration at Corinth (I Cor. 3:4–6; 3:22; 4:6; 16:12) but also as a missionary at Ephesus and perhaps elsewhere (Acts 24–28; 19:1) Titus 3:13). He is sometimes regarded as the author of the book of Hebrews.[8]

The author of the book of Hebrews wrote (2:3): "It was declared at first by the Lord, and it was attested to us that heard him." This strongly suggests that the author had not heard Jesus himself and thus was of the second generation of Christians. It might just possibly mean that

31

the author had not heard Jesus give his particular message of salvation through belief in Jesus himself, even though the author had heard Jesus before the Mission. In any case, it would be most difficult to distinguish in Hebrews even if Apollos wrote it, what he had been thinking before the Crucifixion, so dominant is the thought of that event in the book. There is, however, one short passage (13:1–5) which might illustrate early thought of the author:

> Let brotherly love continue. Do not neglect to show hospitality to strangers ... Remember those who are in prison--Let marriage be held in honor among all - - -. Keep your life free from love of money, and be content with what you have: for he has said, "I will never fail you nor forsake you."

The admonition about money has a peculiarly Epicurean cast, and one notices no reference to special subjection of women to men.[9] With this the possibility is left, remote as it is, that this was the work of Apollos.

The intellectual outreach of Jesus has been indicated by his conciliatory attitude toward the Empire. The eventual triumph of Christianity must have been partly based upon a set of beliefs which could be accepted by the Roman world. This compatibility has been obscured by the apparent hostility of Church and Empire produced by the oath of loyalty to the emperor, which Christians usually refused to take. This oath was a rather artificial barrier between the two, since, except for this refusal to reverence the emperor, Christians would have felt at home with most Romans, especially with the Epicurean element, which was very strong.

Finally, it would have been difficult for Jesus to have acquired the cosmopolitan outlook which he had from within the confines of Palestine itself. Broad-minded as many of the leading Jews doubtless were, they would hardly have accepted the Empire as Jesus did. It is even doubtful if they would have shared his acceptance of the idea of a wealth which should be distributed among the needy, a typical Epicurean principle. Nor, indeed, was there among them the indifference to possessions contrasting with intensity of belief in religious principles. This was, however, just the sort of attitude which a man of wealth, Jew or Greek, might develop under the impact of Epicurean philosophy or its direct influence.

IV

The Baptism and the Temptations

The baptism and the temptations constitute a key
chapter in the life of Jesus of Nazareth, as they would in
the life of any religiously minded leader. As they stand in
the New Testament, they provide an enigma. How could
a village carpenter with little previous experience in the
religious world have suddenly appeared, to be hailed by a
respected prophet, John the Baptist, as "one greater than
myself" and then launch upon a career which changed
the world? One answer, of course, is that it was a religious miracle: this is the orthodox answer. A second
could be, and it would be a good one, that genius cannot
be explained or anticipated. A third is that the earlier and
unknown career of Christ had prepared him for his ministry in Palestine and had even made him known to John
the Baptist. It is this third alternative that is here presented as being a natural and impressive explanation of
what happened. The temptations need to be examined
carefully with respect to the situation presented by the
readings upon which Jesus is said to have been meditating.

"John the Baptizer appeared in the wilderness, preaching a baptism of repentance for the forgiveness of sins"
(Mk. 1:4). A typical Jewish prophet, John drew to himself a multitude of people from a considerable distance.

He aroused the antagonism of Herod the Tetrarch for ob-
jecting to Herod's marrying his brother's widow (Mk. 6:
14–29; Mt. 14:1–12; Lk. 9:7–9), and was beheaded for
his objection. John's movement nevertheless continued
for a century or so. As a prophet first and then a martyr,
he naturally made a tremendous impression upon many,
Jesus among others. John's benediction would be sought
by one preparing a mission parallel to his in Galilee.
And after John's death Jesus fell heir to part of his
movement, even in Samaria and Judea. But before Jesus commenced his career, he experienced a long and
searching meditation in the wilderness. Did it precede
or follow his baptism?

The two stories of the baptism create a problem.
Mark (1:1–12) tells how Jesus was baptized and then
went into the wilderness to meditate. On the contrary,
John gives almost a day-by-day account of Jesus and
John at the time of the baptism (1:19–42), in which Jesus apparently left immediately after the baptism to begin
his Mission. This suggests that Jesus had had his temptations before he was baptized: it suggests that Jesus was
before John on several separate days. Two reasons make
the second seem more probable. The first is that baptism
was a very, very serious act in the ancient world and implied normally that a person had made a great decision in
respect to his religious life. The second is that such a
decision should have preceded rather than followed his
conversion. Thus it seems best to assume that Jesus heard
John and perhaps even heard John speak about him, and
then went to meditate a period of time. After this he returned to John, perhaps from the direction of Nazareth,
was baptized, and then proceeded on his mission.

The story of the baptism is that John almost refused
to baptize Christ because "I need to be baptized by you

and yet you come to me!" (Mt. 3:13–14). But when John was in prison, he sent his disciples to say to him, "Are you he who is to come or shall we look for another?" (Mk. 11:2–3). The two stories are difficult to reconcile as they stand. The general tendency of hagiography is to alter a story already existing: in this case one would expect that John's salutation to Christ would merely be changed rather than an entirely different one substituted. Had John mentioned that he had heard of Jesus' work, his remarks could have been improved upon without great difficulty. It is more likely that John the Baptist would have spoken of Jesus as one to watch if he had had a career of importance outside of Palestine of which John knew. Nor is it surprising that John knew, if Jesus was a relative, as is indicated by the story of John's birth (Lk. 1:36). If such men as Apollos had already been with Jesus and had reported to John, if that is what had happened, one can understand that John would expect great things of Jesus.

The temptations have aroused singularly little comment, although they should occupy a strategic and important position in the life of Christ. The main reason for this is that the absence of information about his earlier life offers little upon which a discussion could be based. Normally, a temptation involves a decision either to continue life as before or to select one of several possible alternatives of action. Thus, if a hypothesis of Jesus' early life is set up, it is possible to have a hypothesis of the nature of the temptation. If we may assume that in his later thirties Jesus had attained wealth and was deeply interested in religion, both Hebrew and pagan, the alternatives should stand out more clearly. He would be in the position of Zeno, who shifted from such a career to found Stoicism, or Mohammed, who gave more and more attention to religion until he established Islam. Peter Waldo, the founder of the Waldensians and perhaps even Francis of Assisi (assuming that he devoted at least a part of his youth to his father's business) would also fall in this class of men of wealth who turned to religion. In fact, the chance of a wealthy merchant taking such a role was more likely than for a village carpenter to do it.

There may have been another factor in his later life, a suggestion presented hesitantly. It is that Jesus was in bad health at the time and that this introduced an element of urgency in his choice. This idea is based upon a series of indications. The first is that the Mission lasted less than a year, and thus one condition of health may be assumed for the whole period. At the end he died on the cross in a few hours, although most men suffered through a much longer period and had to be killed by breaking their legs. He was apparently too feeble to carry the crossbar of the cross (as was customary) to Golgotha, or even answer Pontius Pilate effectively earlier that day. He spoke in the last week of his approaching death, which is assumed to anticipate his crucifixion, but may be merely evidence of serious illness. The gift of perfume is more readily understood if one can assume that the woman saw in Jesus himself signs of approaching death Mk. 14:3–9; Lk. 7:37–38; Jn. 12:3–8). If he had what was the most common sickness of the period, tuberculosis, he could have detected its symptoms long before his decease. "And being in agony he prayed more earnestly; and his sweat became like great drops of blood falling on the ground" (Lk. 22:44). Early tradition as reported by Irenaeus called him "infirmus" (*Haer.* 4:33; 12: 3: 19: 1–2).

Of the temptations Mark (1:13) says only that Christ was in the wilderness forty days, tempted by Satan.

Besides this brief statement there are two sets of explanations in Matthew (4:1–11) and in Luke (4:1–13): the alleged temptations and the Biblical texts upon which Christ based his answers. We may presume that, since he was alone at the time, he repeated to others the nature of his meditations. Taken without their Biblical text they are that (1) he would turn stones into bread because he was hungry, that (2) he would worship or reverence the devil in order that he might rule the world, and that (3) he would jump off of the pinnacle of the Temple in order to show his divine powers. These explanations are not very flattering to Christ's intelligence or conscience: in fact, one might well wonder why he spent more than a few minutes, let alone forty days, on these questions. It is easy to question their validity. Indeed, one has the suspicion that they are poor guesses based upon cryptic references by Christ to the quotations in Deuteronomy upon which he was actually meditating.

All three quotations are from the section of Deuteronomy in which Jehovah is admonishing the Jews as to their attitude once they are in the promised land. The verses in which the last two quotations appear illustrate the situation (Dt. 6:10–16):

> And it shall be, when Jehovah thy God shall bring thee into the land which he sware unto thy fathers, to Abraham, to Isaac, and to Jacob, to give thee great and goodly cities, which thou buildest not, and houses full of all good things, which thou fillest not, and cisterns hewn not, which thou hewest not, vineyards and olive trees, which thou plantest not and thou shalt eat and be full; then beware lest thou forget Je-

hovah, who brought thee forth out of the land of Egypt, out of the house of bondage. Thou shalt fear Jehovah thy God; and him shall thou serve and shall swear by his name. Ye shall not go after other gods, the gods of the people who are about you; for Jehovah thy God is a jealous God; lest the anger of Jehovah thy God be kindled against thee, and he destroy thee from the face of the earth. Ye shall not tempt Jehovah your God as ye tempted him in Massah.

Israel is being admonished upon its conduct once it has become wealthy in the land of Canaan. Christ, if he had acquired wealth, thus was in much the same position, and he would do well to meditate upon the dangers inherent in such a situation.

The first temptation is described thus: "And he ate nothing in those days; and when they were ended, he was hungry. The devil said to him, 'If you are the son of God, command this stone to become bread.' And Jesus answered him, 'It is written, "Man shall not live by bread alone"'" (Lk. 4:3–4). And Matthew adds to the quotation "But by every word that proceeds from the mouth of God" (Mt. 4:3–4). The quotation from Deuteronomy (8:3) says that God furnished manna in the wilderness but did not let the Jews know, lest they be satisfied with it alone. Suppose, however, that Christ was meditating upon the disposition of his wealth. The word "stone" in the Greek can mean "jewel" also, and might refer to wealth, a word which, as we have seen, turns up at least twice in Christ's sayings. If Christ merely gave money for charity (bread), he would still be neglecting "every word that proceeds from the mouth of God." Charity would not be enough: he would use his wealth in a mission to save humanity. His treasurer, Judas Iscariot, could understand charity, but not, apparently, other aspects of his Mission (Jn. 12:4).

The order of the other two temptations differs in Matthew and Luke: probably the order does not matter, since both have to do with problems which would arise in his ministry once he had settled that question. We begin with the one which requires least explanation, that he jump off the pinnacle of the Temple (Mt. 4:5–7; Lk. 4:9–12). "Then the devil took him to the holy city, and set him on the pinnacle of the temple, and said to him, 'If you are the Son of God, throw yourself down; for it is written, "He will give his angels charge of you" and "On their hands they will bear you up, lest you strike your foot against a stone."' Jesus said to him, 'Again, it is written, "You shall not tempt the Lord your God."'" The quotation in Deuteronomy (6:10–16) refers to the tempting of Jehovah at Massah (Ex. 17:7). There, after Israel threatened Moses for lack of water, Jehovah responded by producing water where Moses struck the rock. "And he (Moses) called the place Massah and Meribah, because of the striving of the children of Israel and because they tempted Jehovah, saying, Is Jehovah among us or not?" Miracles, then, were not to be used to prove the existence of God. They might, we presume, be used for the benefit of mankind. It was common practice for followers of the gods to offer miracles to prove the truth of their divinity.

The third temptation presents a more difficult problem (Mt. 4:8–10; Lk. 4:5–8). Again the devil took Jesus to a very high mountain and showed him all the kingdoms of the world and the glory of them; and he said to him, "All these I will give you, if you will fall down and worship me." Then Jesus said to him, "Begone, Satan, for it is written, You shall worship the Lord your God, and

40

him only shall you serve." The term "worship" can be used in the less emphatic sense of "reverence." The problem may well have been that of the group to whom Jesus would address his Mission. If he would make some sort of accommodation with the Roman Empire (Satan often referred to the Emperor), he might attempt to convert the Roman (heavily Epicurean) world by altering its attitude toward God and immortality with some adjustment in morality. Something like this did eventually happen. Perhaps a gesture of reverence toward the Roman Emperor or an acknowledgement that the pagan gods were merely faulty attempts to understand real divinity. After all, Christ quoted a reference in Scripture (Ps. 82:6) in which "Ye are gods" was applied to human beings (Jn. 10:34). The nearness of the Epicurean world of thought to that of Christ would have made this a peculiarly attractive program. The possibility, however, was set aside. Christ would adhere strictly to the Jewish concept of God.

That the relationship of the civil government to religion concerned him more than the few references about it would indicate is shown by the number of quotations from the book of Daniel which appear in his sayings. For Daniel was interested largely in this very question. While Christ solved the question with his statement "Render unto Caesar the things that are Caesar's and unto God the things that are God's," it left open the question of what belonged to each, a question that the confusion common to the world of the emperor and that of the divine made very serious.

If we accept this construction of the temptations (leaving out the devil and assuming meditations on three great problems), we can understand why Jesus devoted forty days to them. The ordeal of deciding to give up his wealth is possibly reflected in his tortured remark about the difficulty of a rich man's entering the kingdom of

41

Heaven equaling the passing of a camel through the eye of a needle. In the ancient world the temptation to perform miracles to make religious truth appear valid was always strong. The possibility of making some accommodation to secular authority to convert the world to his way of thinking must have been peculiarly difficult. Could one depart ever so slightly from the strictest form of worship of Jehovah in order to bring to the world the peace and happiness of the religion of the brotherhood of man? One could argue that it was by refusing to live up to Christ's high standard of divinity (that is, by accepting Christ as divine) that Christianity did conquer the world.

Following these decisions, it was natural that Christ should turn to Palestine and especially to his native Galilee. His message is stated thus (Mk. 12:28–31) Upon being asked,

> "Which commandment is the first of all?" Jesus answered:
> Hear, O Israel: "The Lord our God is one; and ye shall love the Lord your God with all your heart, and with all your soul, and with all your mind, and with all your strength." The second is this, "You shall love your neighbor as yourself." There is no other commandment greater than these.

In contrast with the many divinities worshiped in the great cities, only Jehovah was worshiped in Palestine among the Jews. And in the villages there lived a people who, for the most part, loved their neighbors. This, again, was in contrast with the attitude of the city, with its attention to social distinctions and impersonal indifference to poverty and illness. Especially in his native Galilee would his people understand him and his message. He would be going home.

V

The Length in Time of the Mission

For the length in time of the Mission of Jesus two radically different estimates are made: a little less than a year and a period of three or more years. The difference between the two is very important for our understanding of the Mission. From the standpoint of the disciples, it is the difference between going to school for a single year and finishing a course of three or more years. Few teachers of the ancient world would have thought one year sufficient for even well-prepared students to master their ideas of a total philosophy. The disciples, with possibly some exceptions, were hardly well prepared, and probably could not follow Jesus uninterruptedly through the Mission.

The shorter estimate is essentially that of the Synoptic Gospels: Matthew, Mark, and Luke. In them the two divisions chonologically are the final stay at Jerusalem and an earlier period which might well have been a matter of months.[1] Christian writers Clement of Alexandria, Origen, and Tertullian—who lived early enough to have shared in Christian tradition outside the Gospels, favored the period of only a year, in spite of the fact that they knew the Gospel of John, from which the longer estimate has been made. The normal tendency of tradition would be to extend and make more important the Mission of Christ, so that, if one had to choose on the

43

basis of probability, he would prefer the shorter to the longer estimate of time. This brings us squarely to the problem: why should a chronology be chosen from the Gospel of John?

This choice is based upon the theory that the author of John did have in mind a chronology framed in a successive series of Jewish feasts. These are the Passover (2:13), Passover (2:23), a Feast of the Jews (5:1),[2] the Passover (6:4); Feast of Tabernacles (7:2), the great day of the feast (7:37), Feast of the Dedication (10:22), six days before the Passover (12:1), before the feast of the Passover (13:1). If one assumes that this is a chronological arrangement, then the appearance of at least three Passovers would indicate action in three years. However, there are complications. The cleansing of the Temple which the Synoptics associate with the Passover in which Jesus was crucified, John places just after the mention of the first Passover (2:14—17). Also early in John (4:35) is the indication that he is speaking "yet four months, then comes the harvest," thus placing the time in January or February in Samaria, which Luke, at least, would suggest was the winter before the Crucifixion. The first item, and possibly the second, suggest that the indications of time are not signposts of an absolute chronology but merely suggestions of when, during a year or the year, certain events took place. As such they are valuable, both as actual indications of time during that year and also as showing that Christ went to Jerusalem several times during the Mission. As a deeply concerned Jewish religious leader, he might well have been expected to do this, even though he is not credited with doing so in the Synoptics.

The evidence of the limits of the time of the Mission is uncertain regarding the end due to the difficulty of the

44

Jewish chronology. If one accepts the better evidence from John that the Crucifixion took place on a Friday, the 14th of Nizen, the finding of such a coincidence should settle the question. At least one authority feels that such a coincidence occurs on April 3, A.D. 33.[3] The beginning seems more certain. John is said to have begun his preaching and baptizing in the 15th year of Tiberius (Lk. 3:1), which runs from September 19, A.D. 28 to the same day of the next year. This must have preceded the conversion of Jesus. The first evidence of Jesus' preaching appears in the time of the harvest which, in Galilee, is late May and early June. One might assume, I believe, that Jesus (and probably John) had been in Jerusalem at the Passover that year and that Jesus' meeting with John followed. The Temptation, if at all near six weeks, would have taken the better part of April. The most probable limits for the Mission would then be between the May of A.D. 32 and the Passover of the following year, perhaps eleven months.

For two reasons it is difficult to relate statements and events to particular times and places. The first is that Jesus doubtless stressed the same ideas several times in the course of the ministry. His disciples must have heard him repeat these, and may even have found it difficult to remember just when he presented an idea first or most effectively. This might result in different times for a saying according to the tradition which survived. In the second place, the memory of the people would vary in accuracy with the previous acquaintance with the countryside. Those who heard and remembered were apparently Galileans—at least, in the Synoptics such disciples as are given home places mostly come from that area. It is thus only natural that they would remember most easily the places in Galilee, where they had spent time, and found

45

it less easy to recall in just which villages in Samaria or Judea Jesus had taught. This may account for what seems a fading out of information between the early visits in Galilee, ending with the trip to Sidon and the return, and the entry into Jerusalem through well-remembered Jericho and Bethany. On the other hand, John is centered in Jerusalem and the south, and the area to the north fades out. As a result, Samaria lies in the faded area between the two, and action there is vague, even though probably as much time was spent there as in Jerusalem and its environs or in Galilee.

The first phase of the Mission was apparently from the time that John was arrested, an event which seemingly led to the beginning of Christ's preaching in Galilee (Mk. 1:14–15), and the death of John, which, according to tradition, occurred on August 29. John does suggest that Jesus was teaching and almost competing with John the Baptist before the latter was arrested (3:22–36), but this section looks like an attempt to subordinate the work of John to that of Jesus. It conflicts with the statement in Luke (7:18–23) and Matthew (11:2–15) that John in prison doubted the work of Jesus and sent his disciples to find out about it. It would seem then that, following the arrest of John, probably in April or May, Jesus went to Galilee and began his Mission. Despite John the Baptist's difficulties with Herod Antipas, Jesus' relations with him seem to have been satisfactory. One of his closest women disciples was Joanna, wife of Chuza, the steward of Herod, who stayed with him to the end (Lk. 8:2; 24:10;) and may have been responsible for some of the unusual information in Luke. Jesus himself seems to have remained in Galilee for some time after the beheading of John. Here is another case where it seems that Jesus may have had some relations with government before he began his Mission and therefore was less suspect than he might otherwise have been.

Jesus seems to have hesitated after the death of John the Baptist and Herod's possible hostility attitude toward himself at the time. Perhaps the experience of his rejection at Nazareth and the attitude of his family that something was wrong with him increased his hesitancy. The Gospel of John says that Jesus' brothers went to the Feast of the Tabernacles at Jerusalem in October but still did not believe in him (7:1–8). Jesus followed, apparently taught, and got into an argument with the Pharisees over the keeping of the Law (7:19–24), as well as over the nature of his authority. Mark (7:1–23) places such a discussion with the Pharisees and Scribes "from Jerusalem" in Galilee, but this may be a case where John is the more accurate. John's account of the Jews' conjecturing that Jesus intended "to go to the Dispersion among the Greeks and teach the Greeks" (7:35) did precede a long journey north to the parts of Sidon and perhaps Sidon itself. This was followed by visits to Caesarea, Philippi, and other sites north and along the Sea of Galilee (Mk. 7:24 ff.), and a return to Capernaum (9:33). From this point, accuracy of location largely disappears. Perhaps he went to Samaria at this time: he was accused (Jn. 8:48) of being a Samaritan in a passage, it would seem, before a record of being at Jerusalem at the Feast of Dedication in early December (Jn. 10:22–23).

The last phase of Jesus' life would appear to have been spent in Samaria and Judea. John has the story of the Samaritan woman (4:1–42), which is defined in time by the statement that there is yet four months to the harvest (4:35), and his stay there was regarded as a success in terms of belief of the people. The time, as mentioned earlier, would probably be in January. The incident is localized at Sychar near Samaria, not far from Aenon, where John the Baptist did his baptizing. A great block of chapters in Luke (9:51–18:35) seems to have a certain unity. Three times a going to Jerusalem is mentioned (9:51; 13:22; 17:11) as if this section represents one missionary trip. Capernaum is definitely left behind (10:15); the Galileans at Jerusalem are mentioned as if Jesus is in neither place (13:1). The story of the bad Samaritan village (9:51) is followed soon by the story of the Good Samaritan (10:29–37). Of ten men cured, only a Samaritan gives thanks (17:16). There are two items which suggest that Jesus may have returned to Galilee just before going to Jerusalem the last time. The mention of the last journey says that "passing along between Samaria and Galilee" (17:11), he entered a village; and the statement alleged by some Pharisees that Herod wished to kill Jesus rather suggests that he was still in the jurisdiction of Herod, which would not include Samaria (13:31).

The lack of place names reduces one to conjectures about where Jesus was, even assuming that he was largely in Samaria (and Judea) in the winter of A.D. 33. The gospel of St. Luke tells of his being in a village (9:52; 10:38; 17:11) and at a synagogue (13:10). However, the latter rather suggests a city. Several stories perhaps indicate the audience of a city with tales which should interest urban people: the judge in a certain city (18.2), rich men (16:1,19), tax collectors and sinners (15:1), even the Prodigal Son (15:11–32). "What king" might well be appropriate for Caesarea on the sea, the Roman capital in the area (15:31). With him at the time were at least John (9:49; 10:54), James (10:54), and Peter (18:28). One can hardly miss the large number of stories which have an intrinsic interest for women (among others 10:38;

11:27; 11:29; 12:22; 13:10; 15:8; 18:15), of which that of Mary and Martha is the most telling in its high estimate of women. All of this suggests that perhaps Joanna, wife of Chuza, was the source of many of the items concerning the winter of the year. Just as Jesus seems to have used Capernaum in the north as a sort of center, it would have been probable that he stayed longest at Samaria and Caesarea, although the later attitude of Pontius Pilate rather tends to eliminate Caesarea.

The interpretation of the year of the Mission, assuming that it was only a year, thus rests upon a series of hypotheses, some fairly well founded, some highly conjectural. Essentially it assumes a summer around the Sea of Galilee, a fall traveling about central and northern Galilee and its environs, and a winter largely in Samaria, with some time in Judea and possibly a trip to Galilee. This should have left two centers in which he had friends and followers: near Capernaum and in Samaria, perhaps along the coast. In addition, if the Gospel of John is correct, he would have spent some time in Jerusalem, a place which he might well have known from an earlier period. Despite occasional statements about large numbers in his audiences, it seems likely that the number of his followers was quite limited, and there are suggestions that they were not entirely convinced or at least were not certain just what Jesus' position was at the time.

IV

The Mission

Few topics have evoked as much discussion, with as wide a variety of conclusions, as that of the Mission of Christ. The point of view expressed here is that Jesus commenced his Mission, not as a religiously-minded carpenter from Nazareth, but as a rather sophisticated and wealthy person from the Dispersion, giving his life to spread his doctrine of the love of God to his fellow Galileans. He may even have been ill at the commencement of his Mission and thus have felt a sense of great urgency with respect to time. It is partly for this reason that one is inclined to feel that any choice in the estimate of the time of the Mission should be given to the shortest. A second reason for this choice is that Jesus' followers failed to understand his objectives in many respects, again suggesting that lack of time was one important factor in this failure. The purpose of the Mission, as indicated by instructions to the apostles, was to preach the kingdom and to heal the sick (Mk. 3:14). "And he sent them out to preach the kingdom and to heal" (Lk. 9:2).

Christ returned to a society intensely interested in religion and very receptive to new ideas in regard to it. Within the society of the Jews there were many divisions. The Pharisees, although spoken of harshly in the Gospels, actually seem to have been closer to Jesus in his attitude toward society than the Sadducees, who were intensely conservative. The latter were largely in charge of the official activities of the Jewish religion: sacrifices, ritual, even civic administration. Then there were the Essenes, practically a monastic group, the discovery of whose library at Qumran has recently aroused intense interest. The Zealots were superpatriots of the period. John the Baptist had just commenced a revival campaign for more earnest religious life: repent and live a proper life. The way was thus open for religious innovation of many types within the general field of Jewish beliefs. The religious and secular activities of Palestine had repercussions throughout the Roman world at the time. The triumph of the empire had much reduced the emotional outlets provided by city-state warfare: this emotional vacuum was easily filled by religious beliefs which, like the Empire, were apt to be widely based.

This very intensity of religious interest made the question of the method of propagating his message less important than might have been the case in an area of less religious feeling. Jesus could count upon the spread of ideas if they caught on at all. So it seems that only the most elemental efforts were made toward what we should call organization. He taught in the synagogues, reading the lessons and leading such discussion as followed. Eventually the continuity of Jewish example led to the Christian form of worship, which resembled that of the Jews in some ways. Jesus held meetings in the homes of friends and acquaintances. "For where two or three are gathered in my name, there I am in the midst of them" (Mt. 18:20). On occasion he spoke from the hillsides to great groups of people. He even had a small group of special followers, the twelve who were disciples. Yet the exact list varied:

several hardly appear at all in later Christian activities, and any formal organization or activity as a group is difficult to describe. Jesus seems to have had no name for the movement, if we may call it that.

The loose association of small groups gave place after the Crucifixion to more tightly organized groups in the cities as they waited for Christ to return. It would be hard to claim originality for so universal an organization as an informal small group in the ethnic quarter of a particular city or in a village: it is too natural a development. However, the example of the most effective philosophical group, the Epicureans, must have had some influence: it apparently consisted of small groups meeting in homes and holding a special meal in the founder's honor on the twentieth of each month. It is another case where the early Christian development paralleled that of Epicureanism.

These groups were apparently unrelated except by the visits of Jesus and his followers. Their center, or at least where Jesus visited most in the summer and fall, would seem to have been Capernaum, at the north end of the Sea of Galilee. Here he is mentioned as the guest of Zebedee and his sons, and here he returned a number of times from his trips.[1] If he was residing in Palestine, he might have been expected to have a more permanent home, perhaps at Cana, where his mother lived, or at Nazareth. The lack of a permanent residence again would suggest that he was living outside of Palestine immediately before the Mission.

Jesus apparently began his Mission by following his early habit of speaking in the synagogues, but changed his message. Early Christians, of course, continued with this custom for some time, since they felt that they were still Jews. After all, there were many groups in the Hebrew religion who adopted usual forms of worship and even unusual ideas of theology. Jesus, like later Christians, found himself rejected in many places. The first to be mentioned was probably Nazareth. The "woes" to Chorazin, Bethsaida, and Capernaum (Lk. 10:13–15) show that he had been rejected there. This probably resulted in a denial of the use of the synagogue, and forced him to do his teaching in homes and in the fields. His following thus became much more personal in their adherence to him as the separation from the orthodox practices grew.

If the continuity of the Mission was set up in the rather tenuous form of a committee of twelve meeting occasionally with local groups, operating mainly through synagogues, the message apparently was largely expected to continue as an unorganized body of sayings. John the Baptist, it was said (Lk. 11:1), gave his followers prayers to say; apparently as a result of this Christ gave an outline of a short prayer, the Lord's Prayer, since universally used by Christians. The Last Supper was eventually to be a regular rite, but its beginning was tenuous, and one suspects that its similarity to the Epicurean monthly feast made it a fixed feature among the Christians. Eventually, also, certain features of the Jewish service continued even after the Christians separated completely from the Jews, an event which seems to have come rather more quickly than might have been anticipated.

At first sight one might think that the lack of a definite organization and of a standard set of rites or ceremonies might be a handicap. In the long run it was the source of great strength; each generation, even each group of Christians, has found the precedents of the Gospels so vestigial and so simple that it can set up its own form of organization and believe that it is "primitive Christianity revived." And the Church itself could read into the oracular remarks of Christ the meaning which serves as a justification of the supremacy of the Papacy or of the importance of the patriarchates.

Two possible reasons for the inchoate state of organization or ceremonies exist. The first is that Christ wished it this way: that he thought great ideas have an existence of their own which will spread through their greatness and develop an institutional expression naturally in the course of time. The other possible answer is that he did not have time to do these things: that he died too soon. Suppose, for instance, that Mohammed had died in the Hegira: what would Islam have been like without the system that Mohammed built for his sect in the last ten years of his life?

Every prophet had, of course, his teaching methods, which involve the forms of presentation of material. Christ began with the Law, which not only was well known in the villages in which he visited but also was a favorite with him. One obvious method, then, was commenting upon outstanding texts of Scripture. In addition to the Pentateuch, he liked, as did all Jews, the Psalms. He was especially fond of Isaiah and Daniel, and used stories from them frequently. His interest in these apocalyptic utterances suggests that they inspired him to pour forth the sayings which are attributed to him on the Mount of Olives (Mk. 13).

Some of his sessions were in the nature of question-and-answer periods. Indeed, many of his remarks which are not so indicated may also have originally been of that character. This form of instruction would account, in part, for the rather haphazard form of the teachings as they have come down to us. Unlike Epicurus, Jesus did not provide well-thought-out outlines of his beliefs. He drew from his knowledge of Law and his conception of religion as he needed. The question of why no formal outline was made naturally arises. One possible answer is that he wished his followers to master the central beliefs, which were relatively simple, and then apply them as necessary. Another answer is, of course, one that comes naturally in view of the short course of his mission: that he died before he got around to it.

Because of the nature of his teaching Jesus must have said certain things a good many times in a good many places. The recollections thus must result in a miscellaneous series of stories. The problem of the collector was a problem of organization, both of subject matter and of place of delivery. It would be natural to associate the Beatitudes (Mt. 5:3–12; Lk. 6:20;–26), whether they were given at one place and time or whether they were simply gathered from various times and places. Similarly, the "woes" (Mt. 23:13–39) fall easily into a group, as do the parables. It is not suprising, then, that since there was little significant about the villages in which Christ taught, the course of the journeys themselves should have left little impress as compared with the teachings. Indeed, one of the chief differences between the Mission in the villages and in Jerusalem is in the type of questions discussed in the two places.

The results of his teaching show that Jesus was a superb teacher. Although he wrote down none of his sayings, his followers remembered a long series of his teachings, even making allowance for the custom of the ancient world to retain more in memory than we do today. There is an alternate possibility that Matthew did write down many of Jesus' words. Not only were his words remembered, but they were the basis of the thought and action of his followers, who drew constantly larger numbers to them. The methods by which he attained his results are thus of some importance.

The Beatitudes and "woes" illustrate one type of teaching: the presentation of ideas in a form which enables the hearer to preserve them easily in his memory. The "woes" are given only in Luke (6:24–26):

> But woe to you who are rich, for you have received your consolation.
> Woe to you who are full now, for you shall hunger.
> Woe to you who laugh now, for you shall mourn and weep.
> Woe to you, when all men speak well of you, for so their fathers did to the false prophets.

These are set up in pairs of verses, as was typical of Hebrew poetry. In a sense the effect is Greek, in that the vicissitudes of human fate are offered as probable. One is led to expect nemesis.

The version in the Gospel of Matthew (5:3–12) gives only the Beatitudes. The effect of the contrasting fates thus is avoided. In Luke, not only are contrasts given; they are given as an exact parallel in the number (6:20–22):

> Blessed are you poor, for yours is the kingdom of God.
> Blessed are you that hunger, for you shall be satisfied.
> Blessed are you that weep now, for you shall laugh.
> Blessed are you when men hate you, and when they exclude you and revile you, and cast out your name as evil, on account of the Son of man!
> Rejoice in that day, and leap for joy, for behold, your reward is great in heaven; for so their fathers did to the prophets.

56

The extra length of the last beatitude, as compared with the parallel "woe," suggests either later editing or a later version by Jesus.

In Matthew there has obviously been a rearrangement of the sets of verses: the emphasis seems to be upon the individual verses rather than upon their impact in pairs. It suggests that the author was diverging from the original pattern, perhaps because an explanation of the original very simple verses by Jesus had caused the original order to be lost. The "poor" now are explained as the "poor in spirit," and those who "hunger" now are those who "hunger and thirst after righteousness" (Mt. 5:3,6). And evidently others are included. Since "meek" means those who are "well harnessed," one would have expected that the pair of verses would read (Mk. 5:5,9):

> Blessed are the meek, for they shall inherit the earth.
> Blessed are the peacemakers, for they shall be called sons of God.

This includes a wider range of persons than did the version in Luke, for here are included just the types of persons who could be appreciated as movers of everyday life in the Empire. The criterion is thus not success or failure, but the spirit and purpose of the group.

The parables illustrate another type of teaching. Each parable tells a story and emphasizes only one point. Thus the parable of the Prodigal Son is really the parable of the Selfish Brother, who refused to welcome his brother. This parable illustrates the danger of trying to get too much from a single parable. For one might draw from it, if not approval, at least great sympathy, sufficient to encourage others, for the errant prodigal, which certainly Christ did not intend to do. Nor does it approve of the total action of the father, for we can have a certain sympathy for the boy who stayed at home and did the work. The truth is that too little is known of the situation to justify further deductions than that a Christian spirit encourages a welcome to one who has repented. But the story stands out in one's mind: it must have told the story of many young men who left the Palestine villages for the great seacoast cities and came back, facing parental and family disapproval, a disapproval which even Christ must have felt.

If Christ could be clear, he could also be mysterious. Few approaches arouse the interest and draw out the best thinking of men as do mysteries. Epicurus explained the method thus:

> When I speak of nature I should frankly prefer to play the oracle and cover with obscurity the truths useful to mankind, even things no one were to understand me, rather than conform to common opinion and so gather the praise for which the mob is lavish.

It was an approach which appealed to the outstanding minds of the time. Sometimes Christ explained what he had meant, but other times he left the mystery to be solved.

We may wish to ask the question "What made Christ think that the Kingdom of Heaven could be achieved within a short time; perhaps even in his own lifetime?" The hopes and expectations of those who try to reform the world or make a better society are nearly always too rosy with respect to the actual situation. This is a condition which we should know well, especially the older of us. Were we not going to convert the world to Christ in our generation, make the world safe for democracy—and did

we not fight a war to end all wars? In this age of dis-
illusionment, it is easy to forget the overpowering en-
thusiasms of even the early twentieth century.

The second phase of the Mission was that of healing.
The earliest reference in the Synoptic literature seems to
come from Q (to be discussed later) in the report Jesus
is said to have made to the followers of John (Mt. 11:4;
Lk. 7:22): "Go and tell John what you hear and see: the
blind receive their sight and the lame walk, lepers are
cleansed and the deaf hear, and the dead are raised up,
and the poor have good news preached to them." The
ability to heal was one of the qualities of the prophet in
Israel, as in the case of the healing of Naamon by Elisha
(Lk. 4:27). But about the only recorded act in Q of Jesus' curing a person is his cure of the centurion's slave
(Lk. 7:2; Mt. 8:5). In the first version he was at the
point of death, and in the second paralyzed and in terrible distress. The servant, according to the statement, was
healed at Jesus' word even though he had not reached
the place. In John more miracles were mentioned, and
Mark records about eighteen.

The problem of miracles attributed to any religious
leader in the ancient world is difficult. As we have seen,
Jesus recognized in one of the temptations the danger of
association with miracles which merely proved his divine
power. If, as we suspect, Jesus was a physician, there is
the complication of separating what is merely clinical
activity on his part from what is thought to be miraculous.
The third, and probably most difficult, factor was the tendency to attribute miracles to him because he was a
great religious leader. At least, the fact that miracles
were attributed to him is indicative of the high religious
regard in which he was held, the more so since he was ac-
corded the greatest of all miracles, raising the dead.

59

The cult of individuality was strong in the ancient world. When the Greeks felt that a change was needed, they put their trust in a single great reformer:Solon, Cleisthenes, Timoleon. The Romans saw somewhat the same development: Appius Claudius and his changes, the Gracchi who failed, Sulla, Pompey, Julius Caesar, and finally Augustus. In the field of religion and philosophy, great names like Plato, Zeno, and Epicurus dominated the field and effected great and radical changes in the thinking of the people. As mentioned earlier, the lives of thousands of people were changed merely by the example of Epicurus. Probably he would have been Christ's exemplar in leadership: Epicurus had formed small groups who had very strong beliefs, who held a meal in honor of the founder each month, and who looked to him for inspirational direction and encouragement. With some knowledge of the achievements of the great leaders, Jesus of Nazareth had to hope for the success of his Mission to the world.

VII

The Message

The message of Jesus of Nazareth has, almost from the beginning, been intertwined with the question of the nature of the messenger. Even what Christ said about his status as messenger has become a part of the message, the part which has caused endless discussion, controversy, and heresy among Christians from his day to this. The Coptic Gospel of St. Thomas, perhaps of the second century, has the following presentation of ideas about Christ:[1]

> Christ, "Tell me whom I am like."
> Peter, "Thou are like a righteous angel."
> Matthew, "Thou are like a wise philosopher."

Thomas then gave a most mysterious answer, which indicated that the true statement was a terrifying mystery. The problem, then, of the nature of Jesus was an absorbing question for early Christianity, which had to place what Jesus said and did in the religious framework of Jewish and Hellenistic thought at a time when such thought patterns were changing shape and in which an almost incredible variety of religious ideas circulated. With the increasing dominance of the religious in the thought of the world, it was almost inevitable that eventually one religion would win out. Society wants uniformity and intolerance of the nonuniform in the dominant area of thought. Except for the problem of Christ's nature, the message does not seem so difficult to understand.

One of the ironies of Christian history is that a prayer which Jesus gave to his followers to avoid stereotyped prayer has become the standard prayer used by millions of Christians. It appears in two versions, obviously to suggest types of objectives of those who pray.

Pray then like this (Mt. 6:9–13):
Our Father, who art in heaven
Hallowed be thy name.
The kingdom come,
Thy will be done,
   On earth as it is in heaven.
Give us this day our daily bread,
And forgive us our debts,
   As we also forgive our debtors;
And lead us not into temptation,
   But deliver us from evil.

When you pray, say (Lk. 11:2–4):
Father,
Hallowed be thy name.
Thy kingdom come.

Give us this day our daily bread,
And forgive us our sins,
   for we ourselves forgive everyone
   who is indebted to us;
And lead us not into temptation.

Along with the two commandments Jesus gave when asked about the most important ones, this prayer should be the heart of the Christian message.

62

Of the prayer, the first three lines are purely Jewish in background: the first two are essentially the first commandment. The third might well be ambiguous: what was the kingdom, a religious condition or a political state? "On earth as it is in heaven" is quite Epicurean in theology. So also is "Give us our daily bread," since one of Epicurus' conditions for a peaceful mind was sufficient food. Even the forgiveness of debt approaches Epicurean benevolence towards others, although as stated it is probably the most peculiarly Christian part of the prayer. The last two raise a question: how could God lead a person into temptation? In this assumption of a personal God no Epicureanism appears at all. It is indeed a very personal prayer, assuming God's intense interest in each of us.

Christ's message, as he stated it, was that men should love God and their fellow men, and that, as a result, the Kingdom of Heaven would develop on earth. Of course, this involves a variety of details to put the program into action. Jesus was an earnest Jew, had great faith in the Law. "You know the Ten Commandments," he said, as if this was the beginning of wisdom (Lk. 10:26). His optimism and respect for humanity were a part of his Jewish heritage as well. Probably he was acquainted with and appreciated Epicureanism, so close to it were many of his ideas. One element of Epicureanism, the interest in cosmogony, he did not share. Except for an appreciation of the beauty and wonder of nature, Jesus did not delve deeply into it. His attention was concentrated on man rather than upon the mysteries of the universe. To this end he was encouraged by his deep interest in Isaiah, which seems to be quoted or referred to at least two dozen times in verses scattered through that book.[2] He and those who wrote about him were widely acquainted with it, as they were, of course, with the Pentateuch, the

Psalms, and Daniel. In this he was in line with the highest Jewish traditions.

Christ felt that the minutiae of the Law were unnecessary and often got in the way of genuine religion. This appears in his strictures upon insistence on avoidance of humanitarian activities on the Sabbath (Mk. 3:1), on the picking of grain on the Sabbath (Mk. 2:23), and on the failure to wash hands ritually (Mk. 7:1, 14). It was upon such topics as these that Christ differed with the Pharisees and other Jewish leaders. Yet in general his position was very near that of the Pharisees, as opposed, for instance, to the Sadducees, whose center was the Temple and its sacrifices (Mk. 12:34). Nevertheless, Christ did follow the customs of the Jewish religion, and felt that they were good. In this he was like Epicurus, who suggested that his followers join in the usual religious celebrations. There was obviously an area of thought with respect to sacrifices and rites in which Jesus had no strong feelings unless they seemed to hinder humanitarianism, or what he would probably have called the Kingdom of Heaven.

As mentioned earlier, one can expect no well-arranged body of doctrine from Christ. Such an arrangement of teachings as there is, notably in Matthew, must have been largely the work of the compiler. The purpose of the teaching was to hold out to hearers an ideal of thought and action whose details would derive naturally from the principles themselves. The ideal is what Jesus seems to have called the Kingdom of God (Luke) or the Kingdom of Heaven (Matthew). The Gospel of John says little about it, and Mark gives only a few clues: the parable of the distribution of seed and of the mustard seed. That is, that the kingdom was essentially a great idea which, once held, might be expected to grow magnificently under fair

64

circumstances, poorly under bad conditions. Mark was more interested in Christ's career than he was in an outline of the message, except as it was needed in the exposition to follow the career. With a keen sense of good narrative, he did not interrupt the flow of the story with unnecessary intellectual meandering, and certainly not with a well-thought-out exposition of theology. But perhaps he felt that the body of teachings then in circulation did not require such an exposition.

Whatever the kingdom, Christ emphasized the great and almost terrible urgency of seeking it. Matthew gives two parables concerning this (13:44—45):

> The kingdom of heaven is like treasure hidden in a field, which a man found and covered up; then in his joy he goes and sells all that he has and buys that field.
>
> Again, the kingdom of heaven is like a merchant in search of fine pearls, who, on finding one pearl of great value, went and sold all that he had and bought it.

Luke preserves two others (9:59—62):

> To another he said, "Follow me." But he said, "Lord, first let me go and bury my father." But he said to him, "Leave the dead to bury their own dead; but as for you, go and proclaim the kingdom of God." Another said, "I will follow you, Lord; but first let me say farewell to those at my home." Jesus said to him, "No one who puts his hand to the plow and looks back is fit for the kingdom of Heaven."

The chances are that the second set of parables is like the first, rather than being actual happenings. Here, as with all parables, a single point is made to which the rest of the tale is subordinate. It is really difficult to square the apparent harshness of the second two items with Christ's kingdom, and one probably does not need to. Again, like Epicurus, Jesus felt the urge of the present.

The kingdom will apparently come with the conversion of men to a Christian way of action. "Being asked by the Pharisees when the kingdom of God was coming, he answered them, 'The Kingdom of God is not coming with signs to be observed; nor will they say, 'Lo here it is!' or "There!" for behold the kingdom of God is in the midst of you.' "

Certain of the more subtle parables seem to indicate conditions within the kingdom. In the kingdom one will be rewarded according to his willingness to do the will of God, as the householder paid the workers the same whether they worked or waited to work all day (Mt. 20:1–16): the comment that the last will be first misses the mark. The wise maidens were ready for the marriage (Mt. 25:1–13; Lk. 14:16–24), some servants tried to make money with their loaned talents (Mt. 25:14–30; Lk. 19:12–28), those who came (with wedding garments) even though not originally invited were welcome (Mt. 20:1–14; Lk. 14:15–24), and the actions of those who originally refused were commendable beyond those who accepted and did nothing (Mt. 21:28–32). The acceptance of the principles of the Lord was the important factor in action. The result would be like a kingdom of children with their finest qualities evident (Mt. 19:13–15; Mk. 10:13–16; Lk. 18:15–17). Whosoever shall not receive the kingdom of God like a child shall not enter it.

The code of conduct was the typical Jewish code minus the heavy emphasis upon minute regulations of the law. "Good teacher, what must I do to inherit eternal life?" And Jesus said, "Why do you call me good? No one is good but God alone. You know the commandments: Do not kill, Do not commit adultery, Do not steal, Do not bear false witness, Do not defraud, Honor your father and mother" (Mk. 10:17–19). Much the same is stated earlier in Mark (7:20–23): "What cometh out of a man is what defiles a man. For from within, out of the heart of man, come evil thoughts, fornication, theft, murder, adultery, coveting, wickedness, deceit, licentiousness, an evil eye, slander, pride, foolishness. All these evil things come from within, and they defile a man."

The theological concepts even of the Jews made for the possibility of supernatural beings between divinity and humanity. Archangels, angels, and other beings occupied the intervening space in a very undefined way. Isaiah's messenger was one of these, and possibly this was most in the mind of the day. Here language was one of the problems. The Semites did not like to define divinity or supernatural manifestations: they were to be honored and revered, but not separated and given accurate definitions. When Christ spoke of himself as a son of man he probably thought (and this is said most hesitantly) of himself as one who shared in a mystical relationship to the divine and felt especially certain of his knowledge of the divine will. He felt so keenly the divine character of his message that his own character made little difference.

The distinction of this world from the next was not sharp in Christ's thinking. On the one hand, the next world should be brought into this one. "Thy kingdom come; thy will be done on earth as it is in Heaven." Similarly, one will receive reward or punishment in Heaven for one's actions on earth, but the nature of the two is not stated. Like so much else, the nature of the future is not defined in detail. It would take the Middle Ages to try to define Heaven, Purgatory, and Hell so vividly that authors could write books about them. The general principles were outlined, but seldom specific details.

The course to this point could be shared by most Christians, but beyond this, in the realm of the theological concepts associated with Jesus as the Redeemer of Israel and the Savior of the World, the divergence would be great. The field is one of interpretation of ideas, of words, and of the crosscurrents of religious thought of the first century after the Crucifixion. But the message has never been lost: it has been a message of devotion to God and the love of humanity, a message which has animated Christians into humanitarian activities from the time of Jesus to the present.

VIII

The Apostles and Followers

There are, as usual, mysteries about the men whom Jesus asked to be his apostles. The lists place them in a quite definite order which, as we shall see, is probably the order of their seating arrangement, something about which the ancient and medieval world was particular. It is taken up first because it does seem to be definite, and the changes in it may denote chronological rearrangement. Another assumption that seems reasonable is that Jesus knew most of the men before he asked them to join him, and possibly had known them for relatively long periods of time, in spite of the apparent abruptness of the call as given in the Scriptures. Had it been sudden, it should have been remembered more exactly than it was. The sharp divergence of circumstances of the location of the call in Galilee, as in Mark (1:14–20), and at the Jordan, as in John (1:35–51), would show a vagueness of memory concerning the place of the summons. This is probably evidence of long association in which the change from a close friendship (in most cases) to discipleship must have been slow and uncertain.

According to Mark (10:35–45), the sons of Zebedee asked to sit on the right and left hand of Jesus in glory; Matthew (20:20; 28) says that it was their mother, Salome, who asked. In either case a seating arrangement

The Seating Arrangements

Matthew-Mark

Jesus

Simon Peter	James
Andrew	John
Philip	Nathaniel or
Matthew or	Bartholomew
Levi, son of	Thomas the
Alphaeus	Twin
James, son of	Thaddeus
Alphaeus	
Simon the	
Canaanean	

Judas Iscariot

Luke

Jesus

Simon Peter	James
Andrew	John
Philip	Bartholomew
Matthew	Thomas
James, son of	Simon the
Alphaeus	Zealot
Judas, son	
of James	

Judas Iscariot

70

Peter

John		Andrew
James		Philip
Thomas		Bartholomew
Matthew		James, son of Alphaeus
Simon the Zealot		Judas, son of James
Matthias		Simon, called Barsabbas

is assumed, presumably on earth as in heaven, which should be followed in the lists. Actually three lists are given which probably follow a chronological order: Mk. 3:16 and Mt. 10:2–4, Lk. 6:14–16, Acts 1:13. In general, the order of precedence seems to be the same as the order of becoming disciples, modified by family relationships, with the older brother normally preceding the younger. Thus, although Andrew is said to have joined Jesus before his brother, Peter, the latter is given first (Jn. 1:35). Presumably he sat to Jesus' right with Andrew next to him, since brothers usually sat next to each other. After them came James and John presumably sitting to Jesus' left. Then follow four whose places are not so certain, except that Philip is given as the fifth, and thus presumably he sat on the right side next to Andrew. According to John (1:43–51), Philip found Nathaniel of Cana, who followed Christ and who is prominent in John (21:2): the latter is probably surnamed "Son of Tolmai, or Bartholomew," appearing as such in the Synoptic Gospels. Bartholomew, Thomas, and Matthew appear almost indifferently in order, with Thomas gradually rising. James, son of Alphaeus, follows in all the lists, and presumably

71

sat in the fifth position in the right side.

The relationship of these three—Matthew, Thomas, and James, son of Alphaeus—may be that of brothers. In Mark, Matthew is given as Levi, son of Alphaeus, who may be expected to be the same as the father of James. The position of Thomas seems occasionally to be between Matthew and James, which might well be the position of a third brother. Since Thomas is called "the Twin" (Jn. 20:24), one might assume that he was twin of Matthew, who sits next to him at table. Since, as we shall see, much of the information about Jesus probably came from Matthew, it is important to know the character of his family for the light it casts on his point of view. Thomas was also called "the Doubter" because of his attitude toward the Resurrection (Jn. 20:25), indicative of a skeptical type of mind. Matthew himself must have been of an unconventional type of mind to defy the dislike which the Galileans had of tax collectors and to become one. It should mean also that he had some appreciation of the problems of government and of its operation. Luke speaks of the "great feast" which Levi threw when he became an apostle, somewhat unconventional as a exercise of religious conversion, shocking even to the scribes and the Pharisees (Lk. 5:27–39). To do this, Matthew must have been a man of wealth or of considerable means: one who could appreciate what it meant to give up a position of affluence to join the Mission. Obviously the family of Alphaeus, if Matthew, Thomas, and James were his sons, was not a narrow-minded provincial group, but one which was acquainted with and had adjusted to the world. Jesus was fortunate, or perhaps foresighted, to have such a group as the source of information about his Mission.

After these nine, problems arise. The first list gives Thaddeus in the position opposite James, son of Alphaeus, but he is succeeded by Simon the Zealot, presumably Simon the Canaanean of the first list, who has moved up. Although Judas Iscariot is in twelfth place in the first list, he does not move up to eleventh, the place which is taken by Judas, son of James. The moving up would show a chronological change: possibly the order is that of the winter in Samaria and Judea which is stressed in Luke, although the list is given as that of the original group. Perhaps Judas is listed last because he was the betrayer, but possibly it was because he occupied a different position, as the treasurer of the group, sitting, perhaps, at the end of the table. He seems to have been the only non-Galilean in the group. If Jesus was a wealthy man, one is tempted to think that Judas was an associate from the earlier days of money-earning, and never really approved of the Mission. Or, as a non-Galilean he may have felt himself out of sympathy with these less sophisticated persons who surrounded Jesus.

The question of seating on high seems to have been caused by the rise of John in the affection of Christ. If John was actually seated next to Jesus at the Last Supper, he had changed places with his brother James. The request of Salome, if it was she who made it, was that Peter should be demoted from his position at the right hand of Jesus.

The age of the disciples presumably would be the same as that of Jesus or younger. Indeed, both of the parents of James and John, that is, Zebedee (Mk. 1:20) and Salome (Mt. 20:20), were alive, and Peter's mother-in-law was also alive (Mk. 1:30). Andrew, presumably unmarried, lived with his brother Peter, and one doubts whether James and John were married either. The impression is that they were rather young. The families seem to have been living at Capernaum, although Peter and Andrew are said, like Philip, to have come from Bethsaida, at the head of the Sea of Galilee (Jn. 1:44). Nathaniel (Bartholomew) came from Cana (Jn. 21:2), where Jesus' mother was living. That he did not seem to know Jesus is another reason for thinking that Jesus was not living in Galilee at the beginning of the Mission. Peter and James seem to have come from a prosperous family, since their family had servants. Although somewhat mercurial in character, Peter proved to be an excellent leader at a later date. Probably John was the first to understand the real nature of the Mission of Jesus, which may have been the chief reason for Jesus' affection and, apparently, for the family feeling that he should supplant Peter in the seat next to Jesus. Neither Andrew nor James seem to have been outstanding in the early Christian movement.

There seem to have been two occasions when the question of apostolic precedence arose. The first, according to Mark, followed the Transfiguration, and led Jesus to set a child in their midst and declare that one must humble himself to be the leader (Mat. 18:1–4; Mk. 9:33–37; Lk. 9:46–48). The other occasion was the one mentioned earlier: a question whether James and John should not be raised to the top positions (Mk. 10:35–45; Mt. 20:28; Lk. 24:25–30). It was not surprising that this attempt angered the other ten. In fact, a reverberation of this might seem to appear in the order of the apostles given after the Crucifixion (Jn. 21:1–2): Simon Peter, Thomas called the Twin, Nathaniel of Cana, the sons of Zebedee, and two others of his disciples were together. The "sons of Zebedee" are named somewhat contemptuously (I believe), and certainly are set down after Thomas and Nathaniel, who appear below them in the usual lists. And the rather odd scene in John 21:20–22 also shows John in an unfortunate position. "Peter turned and saw following them the disciple whom Jesus loved who had lain close to his breast at the supper and had said, 'Lord who is it that is going to betray you?' When Peter saw him he said to Jesus, 'Lord, what about that man?' Jesus said to him, 'If it is my will that he remain until I come what is that to you? Follow me!'"

Following the death of Jesus and of Judas, a reconstitution of the group would naturally be made (Acts 1:13,23–26). A question arises as to whether Jesus' place at the head was kept vacant or whether Peter moved up to fill it. The arrangement as stated in Acts would suggest that the latter is correct. Peter is given first, followed by John and James. Apparently, then, John did move to Peter's right, and had his brother James at his side. Andrew, as customary, sat next to his brother but at his left. Philip moved to the seat vacated by John and sat next to his friend, Bartholomew-Nathaniel. Thomas technically moved ahead of Matthew, which is easy to explain only if he was Matthew's twin; James, son of Alphaeus, probably Matthew's brother, moved across from Matthew. Simon the Zealot and Judas, son of James, also moved up. Since the list including Jesus had included a thirteenth, one might have expected two more to have been added. Two are considered, but according to Acts, only one was enrolled with the eleven. Shortly after this, the twelve seem to have disappeared as an organization.

Besides the twelve, other men are mentioned as following Jesus. However, women occupied a place rather unusual for a Jewish group: indeed, what is known comes largely from Luke, the most non-Jewish of the Gospels. "The women who had come with him from Galilee followed and saw the tomb" (Lk. 23:55)—they were apparently Mary Magdalene, Joanna, and Mary the mother of James and other women, who returned with the spices two days later (Lk. 24:10). Earlier the list is given (Lk. 8:2) as "Mary, called Magdalene from whom seven demons had gone out, Joanna, the wife of Chuza, Herod's steward and Susanna and many others who provided for them out of their means." The list in Mark at the Crucifixion gives Mary Magdalene, Mary the mother of James the younger and Joses, and Salome, who when he was in Galilee, followed him and ministered to him; and also many other women who came up with him to Jerusalem (16:40–41). The list in John is (19:25) his mother, his mother's sister, Mary the wife of Clopas, and Mary Magdalene. Doubtless, the difference is in the source of information, although they all agree that Mary Magdalene was the most prominent, perhaps the leader. The story of Martha's complaint against Mary (Lk. 10:38–41) would show that the women shared in the religious discussion as well as the men, and did not limit themselves to mere serving. But it is remarkable that none of the women associated with Jesus seem to have been prominent in the development of early Christianity and that the names of the first Christian women leaders are mostly Greek.

Indeed, the Greek element as a whole is one of the mysteries of the period. In the Mission the only Greek contact would appear to be that recorded in John (12:21) of the Greeks who approached Philip and asked to see Jesus. And yet the evidence would show a staunch following among the Hellenists almost from the beginning: the seven leaders of that group (Acts 6:5) included Stephen, the first martyr to the cause, and Philip, the missionary to the Samaritans. Since Peter was hardly enthusiastic about admitting non-Jews to the group, the presence of the Hellenists raises a serious question. Of course, they might have been merely Greek-speaking Jews, but even they must have been subject to a certain amount

76

of missionary work, which assumes either (1) that the apostles spoke Greek, or (2) that the Hellenists had come to believe in Jesus in some other way. Here the possibility arises that the group in part came from those who had been taught by Jesus outside of Galilee before he began his mission there.

The initial center of Christianity was Jerusalem, with James the brother of Jesus as the head. Paul must have shifted the center to Asia Minor-Achaia in much the way Roman governors often moved about their province. If there was a single center, it should have been the metropolis, Ephesus. This shift would doubtless have been aided by the failure of Christ to return, with consequent lowering of the prestige of the people who were awaiting him there. Ephesus became one center, as indicated by the history of the Gospels, which seem to have come respectively from Ephesus, Antioch, Alexandria, and Rome. Whatever chance Jerusalem had of retaining prestige was largely lost by the destruction of the city in A.D. 70. The great unknown in all of this is Alexandria, with its neighbor, Cyrene.

Mark traditionally is believed the founder of Christianity in Egypt, particularly in Alexandria. This was the center of a very large group of Jews, where one might have anticipated a considerable colony of early Christians. Alexandria is hardly mentioned. Instead, Cyrene appears rather prominently in the early Church. It was Simon of Cyrene, father of Alexander and Rufus, who carried the cross of Christ (Mk. 15:21). Among those with the gift of tongues at Pentecost were "residents . . . of Egypt and the parts of Libya belonging to Cyrene" (Acts 2:10). "The synagogue of the Freedmen and of the Cyrenians and of the Alexandrians, of those from Cilicia and Asia arose and disputed with Stephen" (Acts 6:9). Some of these scat-

77

tered because of the persecution of Stephen, "men of Cyprus and Cyrene, who on coming to Antioch, spoke to the Greeks also, preaching the Lord Jesus" (Acts 11:20). "And the hand of the Lord was with them, and a great number that believed turned to the Lord. News of this came to the ears of the church in Jerusalem and they sent Barnabas to Antioch. (6:21). It would appear that this missionary line, apparently a very successful one, from Cyprus and Cyrene was responsible for the Greek element in even Antioch, the place where, it was alleged, Christians were first called by that name (11:26).

Of the Church at Antioch one of the leaders was Lucius of Cyrene, presumably one who had gone to Antioch to teach the Greeks. Now Acts is devoted primarily to the early missions and the work of St. Paul. A look at the map will show that his work lay across Asia Minor and into Greece. It will show also that it did not include Egypt, Cyrene, or, until the end of his life, Rome. Yet his line of missionary endeavor, supported by the Jerusalem group, was constantly crossing that of another stream. We have seen they met at Antioch, where the work of the two was very successful. At Corinth he found a Jew, Aquila, a native of Pontus late came from Rome with his wife Priscilla because Claudius had commanded all the Jews to leave Rome (Acts 18:2–4). At Ephesus he met a Jew named Apollos (who has already been discussed) a native of Alexandria (Acts 18:24), who needed further instruction. At Jerusalem he stayed at the home of Mnason of Cyprus, an early disciple. (21:16).

Or look at the list at the end of the Letter to the Romans (16:7): "Greet Andronicus and Junias, my kinsmen and my fellow prisoners; they are men of note among the apostles and they were in Christ before me." It is hard to imagine any close relatives of St. Paul Christians before he was, so that the relationship may have been distant. Many of the names are obviously Greek, and would seem to imply a considerable missionary effort outside of that of Paul himself. The men in Judaea, with their participation in the Resurrection and close association with Christ, had a very considerable prestige based upon this association. What could have equalized these advantages to give men prestige outside of Judaea? Paul had his experience of revelation from Christ as the base for his activities as one of authority. There is, then, a sort of unknown force existing which needs to be analyzed, which seems to give prestige to men like Apollos and probably to many others. This may well have been association with Christ before his Mission.

IX

The Crucifixion and the Resurrection

The accounts of the last days of Jesus of Nazareth
are very confused. It is clear that he and his followers were
in Jerusalem, that there was some disturbance at the time
of the entry of Jesus on one day, that Jesus was arrested,
tried, and sentenced to be crucified by Pontius Pilate. The
confusion was doubtless caused partly by the scattering of the followers of Christ upon his arrest, so
that there was real doubt about what happened. Then the
Christians tended more and more to dislike the Jews as
the latter refused to join them and even persecuted them.
Furthermore, Christian attitude also turned more favorable to the Romans, especially after the great rebellion at
Jerusalem in A.D. 66—70, a change which tended to put
an unjustifiably favorable light on Pontius Pilate, who
came near being canonized in Egypt. The following is a
reconstruction of events which seems most probable in
view of circumstances in Jerusalem then.

Sometime before the Passover that spring there had
been an insurrection at Jerusalem.[1] It is mentioned in
both Mark and Luke (Mk. 15:6; Lk. 23:19) in connection
with participants still in prison. The Romans had apparently had to smash their way into the Temple area by under-
mining the Tower of Siloam, which fell and killed eighteen people (Lk. 13:5). Probably it was at this time that

Pilate mixed the blood of the Galileans with the sacrifices (Lk. 13:1–2), for doubtless their Zealot propensities caused them to be prominent in the insurrection. What touched it off is uncertain, but the reference to the desolating sacrilege by Jesus (Mk. 13:14) rather suggests that it had been caused by the Romans' bringing their standards into certain parts of the city, which, according to Josephus (*Bell. Jud.* ii, 169–77), had produced intense opposition to Pontius Pilate. Apparently Pilate had left the area before all of the prisoners had been rounded up, and was out of the city at the beginning of the Passover period. The situation was a grim one. One might expect the governor to make an example upon the least possible cause to intimidate the people. This was the condition of the city when Jesus and his followers came into the city: highly explosive, restless, and even dangerous.

Jesus and his disciples had come to Jerusalem a week or so before the Passover, and apparently came in daily from Bethany not far from the city. During these days he taught in the Temple area regularly, as he insisted when he was arrested: "Day after day I was with you in the temple teaching and you did not seize me" (Mk. 14:49). That he was a popular teacher with the crowd of Jews who had come to the city for the Passover seems clear. Had nothing else been done, it is doubtful if Jesus would have suffered.

With the Passover approaching, Jesus and his followers went to the Temple, apparently to buy the sacrificial lamb. The story is recorded thus in Mark (11:7–10):

> And they brought the colt to Jesus, and
> threw their clothes on it; and he sat on it. And
> many spread their clothes on the road and others spread leafy branches which they had cut

from the fields. And those who went before and
those who followed cried, "Hosanna! Blessed be
he who comes in the name of the Lord! Blessed
be the kingdom of our father David that is coming. Hosanna in the highest!"

Both Luke and Matthew emphasize the references to
Christ as king. Such demonstrations were a rather typical feature of Mediterranean life and might be easily
accounted for, under ordinary circumstances, as a simple manifestation of religious enthusiasm. And the reference in Zachariah (9:9) which even then they may have
had in mind—"just and having salvation; lowly and riding
upon an ass, even upon a colt, the foal of an ass"—would
have a religious rather than a political connotation.

In Mark (11:11) it would not appear that much else
happened. "And he entered Jerusalem, and went into the
Temple: and when he looked around at everything, as it
was already late, he went out to Bethany with the twelve."
Odd that it should have been related in this way: it
suggests vaguely that something more had occurred which
the chronicler had omitted. Matthew (21:12) and Luke
(19:45), and thus their common source, tell how Jesus
entered the Temple "and began to drive out those who
sold," and "overturned the tables of the moneychangers
and the seats of those who sold pigeons," saying that his
house should not be made a den of thieves. John (2:15)
even adds that he drove them out with a whip of cords
which he had made.

One can assume, at least, that the procession, possibly
a fairly unruly one, went into the Temple yard, a very large
area. Doubtless the moneychangers and sellers of pigeons
heard the noise of the procession, and fearing what the
mob might do, departed as rapidly as possible. That vio-

lence of the type mentioned happened seems unlikely for at least two reasons. The first is that violence was entirely out of character for Jesus, and the second is that such acts of violence (and probably theft of money from over-turned tables) would have warranted very severe action against Jesus as the leader of the mob. If he had been tried by the Romans for his part in the triumphal entry, many of his followers would certainly have been tried with him. Failure, indeed, to include his followers in Jerusalem indicates that he was tried for some previous act, real or alleged.

Yet even if no violence had been committed by Jesus and his followers, he might well have been called to trial by the Jewish authorities for the procession and resulting disturbance. A trial is mentioned in the Gospels and is set just before the trial before Pontius Pilate. The problem in placing it there is well indicated by the uncertainty whether it was held at night (Mk. 14:53–72; Jn. 18:19–24), which would be most unlikely, or the following morning (Lk. 23:66–71), when the factor of time makes it also improbable. Both times suggest an effort by writers to get in a trial then, in order that the Jews might be saddled with the blame for the Crucifixion, a part of the effort to shift responsibility from the Romans (Mk. 14:55–65). Normally a trial by the Jewish authorities would have followed closely after the incident, instead of several days later. The Jews preferred to handle the cases themselves rather than to let the Romans intrude in their life. In Mark (14:55) there is an interesting statement: "Now the chief priests and the whole council sought testimony against Christ to put him to death and they found none. For many bore false witness against him, and their witness did not agree." The impression given by this statement is that there was a trial of some length and that it led to an acquittal (Lk. 20:39). There would hardly have been time for such an orderly proceeding on the morning of the crucifixion.

If there had been a trial before the Jewish authorities, one might expect that evidence of it would remain. Possibly remains of it appear in the block of verses in the Synoptics (Mk. 11:27–12:37; Lk. 20:1–44; Mt. 21:23–22:48) and in John (18:19–23). Assuming that Jesus was brought before such a court, what questions might be asked? In the triumphal entry he was apparently called a king, which suggested a relationship to David and hinted at the possibility of rebellion against Rome.

Some of the Pharisees and some of the Herodians asked, "Is it lawful to pay taxes to Caesar?" Jesus' answer, "Render to Caesar the things that are Caesar's," was unequivocal, and should have satisfied even the Herodians on the count of possible rebellion (Mt. 22:15–22). The matter of the immortality of the Sadducees follows in the text, but one suspects that it was added to parallel the alleged confusion of the Pharisees. And a second item would suggest that Jesus disclaimed being the son of David (Mt. 22:41–45). These were primarily political questions about which the Jews were properly disturbed, in view of the insurrection some time before. It is understandable for Caiaphas, the high priest, to have said, "It is expedient for you that one man should die for the people and not that the whole nation should perish" (Jn. 11:49–50).

There might have been religious questions as well. "By what authority are you doing these things?" Christ is alleged to have countered by asking by what authority John the Baptist acted—an oblique claim that he acted by the same authority. He placed himself in the prophetic line, a position which the Jews understood and respected. "And one of the scribes came up and heard them ... and

asked him, 'Which commandment is the first of all?'"
Jesus' answer was actually an affirmation of his belief in
the Law, which should have been satisfactory to the group
(Mt. 22:36–40). The version in Matthew is used because
it is the most Jewish in tone and perhaps best represents
what happened. It may be doubted that Jesus asserted
that he was the "son of God" in any sense offensive to the
Jews (Mk. 14:62; Mt. 26:64; Lk. 22:70), because that
would have rendered him guilty of blasphemy and clearly
punishable by death, as the fate of Stephen showed. However, it does seem that the Jews did take some judicial
action and that it resulted in an acquittal of Jesus. Even
with the eventual dislike of the Jewish leaders, the friendship of some of them for Jesus stands out and would
explain why he was given a fair hearing and was freed.

Against the background of the recent trial by the
Jews (assuming that it occurred) and the still remembered insurrection, Jesus' apocalyptic utterances on the
Mount of Olives (Mark 13) would have been peculiarly
appropriate:

> When you hear of wars and rumors of
> wars, do not be alarmed, this must take place,
> but the end is not yet. For nation will rise against
> nation: there will be earthquakes in various
> places, there will be famines; this is but the be-
> ginnings of the sufferings.
>
> But take heed for yourselves; for they will
> deliver you up unto councils; and you will be
> beaten in synagogues and you will stand before
> governors for my sake. And brother will deliver
> up brother to death and father his child and chil-
> dren will rise up against parents and put them
> to death.
>
> But when you see the desolating sacrilege

set up where it ought not to be (let the reader understand) then let those who are in Judea flee to the mountains: let him who is on the housetop not go down nor enter his house, to take anything away. And let him who is in the field not turn back to take his mantle. And alas for those who are with child and for those who give suck in those days. Pray that this may not happen in winter. For in those days there will be such tribulation as has not been seen since the beginning of Creation which God created until now, and never will be.

But in those days after that tribulation, the sun will be darkened, and the moon will not give its light, and the stars will be falling from heaven, and the powers in the heavens will be shaken.

The type is distinctly apocalyptic and again could have been inspired by Isaiah. However, the problem also would be to separate the words which actually were spoken from what might have been added in explanation by some who did not realize what was happening. It seems well within reason that Jesus did utter at least some of the foregoing visions of what might happen, using similar events in the city as illustrations.

During the week Pontius Pilate came to Jerusalem to see that order was kept while the many thousands of Jews were in and about the city, celebrating the Passover. He was probably prepared to intimidate them by trying some of the rebels who were in prison at the time. The Gospels would have it that this powerful ruler released on petition of a group of Jews, because it was the Passover, a man who had committed murder during the insurrection (Mk. 15:7; Lk. 23:19), at a time when such a man would be most dangerous. Furthermore, although he recognized the innocence of Jesus, he allowed him to be brutally beaten, humiliated, and then crucified. All of this seems most unlikely.

Granted that Jesus was crucified as a result of a miscarriage of justice, what happened? Nearly always there is some fairly natural mistake leading to such an act. In this case it may have been the similarity of the names of Jesus Barabbas and Jesus of Nazareth. To judge from the outcry in favor of Jesus Barabbas, he was a popular leader in the city. The move to crucify Jesus of Nazareth may have been primarily to throw upon him the blame that should have been properly attached to Barabbas. Suppose that Pontius Pilate knew only that one Jesus had been responsible for murder and rebellion in the insurrection and was among the prisoners taken, presumably after he had left the city following the rebellion. Might it not be possible for a coalition of Barabbas' sympathizers and dealers in animals and coin in the Temple area to have arranged to arrest Jesus and present him as the Jesus who had caused so much trouble in the rebellion, along with others who would be tried?

Acting on a tip from Judas Iscariot, the officials had Jesus arrested. The group who did it was apparently a cohort of Romans (Jn. 18:3), probably accompanied by friends of Barabbas and adherents of the Temple financiers, who had been worried about Jesus' attitude toward them. He is alleged to have been taken first before the Jewish court, although one would have anticipated that, if taken by order of Pontius Pilate, he would have been carried at once to the Praetorium, where he appears the next day. This may well have been what happened. The story of the hearing before the Jewish authorities is obviously confused: was it in the night or the next morning? The tendency to blame the Jews may have intruded here, since apparently the disciples knew little of what actually happened. One would have anticipated that, if the Jewish leaders had earlier exonerated Jesus, they would have not cared to reopen the case.

Even if the Jews had acquitted Jesus and his followers, there still remained the possibility that the Romans might arrest them for the confusion of the triumphal entry. It was probably this fear that caused the disciples to scatter at the time of the arrest of Jesus, not realizing just what the nature of the arrest was. This, if true, was tragic, for the disciples were the ones who might have saved Jesus from crucifixion by identifying him against the accusations by those who asserted Jesus had been a leader in the insurrection.

Luke tells how Pilate, when he heard that Jesus was a Galilean, turned Jesus over to Herod because Galilee was in Herod's jurisdiction, and that Herod sent him back clothed in purple, believing that Jesus was innocent. However, if it was a question of refusing jurisdiction, two solutions of the return are possible. The first is, of course, that Jesus was accused of something in Jerusalem, which was in Pilate's territory. The second is that Jesus was actually a resident of Roman territory, Judaea, Samaria, or perhaps even Tyre and Sidon. The accusation against Jesus was that he had called himself "King of the Jews." The scene is hard to visualize. On the one hand there is the assertion of people "vehemently accusing him" (Lk. 23:6 —12), the soldiers mocking him and beating him, while on the other hand Herod, and later Pilate, engage in a series of questions, even philosophical in character, with a man who either says nothing or provides seemingly satisfactory answers to the question. Herod was evidently pleased by the courtesy of Pilate asking him about his jurisdiction (Lk. 23:12), if Luke's story is accurate.

In the court before Pontius Pilate a series of men were tried for participation in the rebellion. Jesus' followers were evidently not in the court, since they had scattered at the time of the arrest. He was thus at the mercy of the court. Two others were condemned, and one is alleged to have said "You are under the same sentence of condemnation" to the other, with respect to the sentence of Jesus (Lk. 23:40). The circumstances of his arrest were doubtless suspicious: he was found outside of the city with a group of followers who fled at once. If Peter did perform an act of violence, as alleged, the circumstance was even more suspicious (Mk. 14:47). This may be doubted, since it should have resulted in the immediate arrest of Peter as well as of Jesus. The crowd at the court apparently shouted that the Jesus implicated in the rebellion was Jesus of Nazareth rather than Jesus Barabbas. Even the Galilean background, as indicated by the Galilean speech of Peter and the others, made the identification seem easier: the Galileans were famous for rebellion. Pontius Pilate as a Roman judge doubtless did make an effort to ascertain the identity of Jesus, but found it easier to yield to the crowd than to continue what seemed an unprofitable investigation. But that he was wholly responsible for the verdict is not open to doubt.

That Jesus was already in a bad state of health seems the more likely in view of what followed. Normally, a victim was required to carry the crossbar of the cross: in fact, John says that Jesus did (Jn. 19:17). However, the Synoptic account, being the more unusual, is the more likely. "But as they led him away, they seized one Simon of Cyrene, who was coming in from the country, and laid on him the cross, to carry it behind Jesus (Mk. 15:21; Lk. 23:26). Simon is said to have been the father of Alexander and Rufus, which suggests that they were or became a Christian family. One wonders, perhaps without basis, if Simon of Cyrene really was forced to accept the cross or whether he was an earlier disciple who asked to carry the cross as a last favor. Four times in Acts (2:10; 6:9; 11:20; 13:2) Cyrenians are mentioned prominently among the early Christians, much more prominently than the small population of Cyrenaica should have warranted.

The end came at Golgotha. Forsaken by all but a few, and those mostly women, and possibly suffering from serious illness as well, he was going to die for a crime he did not commit. He had left little in the way of organization and nothing in writing. He might even doubt that his disciples really understood the nature of his mission. He could well wonder if it had been worth the cost to give up a life of respectable ease and affluence and a reputation, possibly, as a religious teacher in the Dispersion for the apparently meagre results and humiliating conclusion of the Mission. No wonder that in his agony he should have chosen as the expression of his feeling the scriptural cry of utter dispair (Mk. 15:34):

My God, why hast thou forsaken me? (Ps. 22:1)

Following its removal from the cross, the body of Christ was claimed by a wealthy leader of the Jews, Joseph of Arimathea (Mk. 15: 42–46; Lk. 23:50–53; Jn. 19:38–41). Nicodemus is said to have brought spices for his burial (Jn. 19:39). The latter is known to have been in touch with Christ during his ministry, but there is no hint that Joseph had been, and one suspects that he may have been a friend of Jesus from earlier days. That he was called "of Arimathea" normally associates him with Greek-speaking areas, where this method of naming was the custom. Joseph apparently placed Jesus in a tomb cut out of the side of hill, perhaps in his private garden, since a gardener is mentioned (Jn. 20:15). "Mary Magdalene and Mary the mother of Joses saw where he was laid" (Mk. 15:47). This implies nothing more than that they saw at some distance where the tomb was. The accounts in Luke and Matthew assume that the women were very close to the tomb (Lk. 23:55; Mt. 27:61).

What happened on the morning when Mary Magdalene, Joanna, Susanna, and perhaps other women sought the tomb of Christ to prepare the body with spices is a great mystery. Apparently, they either found it empty or did not find it at all. St. Paul never mentions the empty tomb: either its significance had not developed yet or it seemed to need no explanation on his part. As one can see from the Gospels, the story took on more details of an increasingly supernatural character. It seems that the importance of the empty tomb derived from the Resurrection, rather than the reverse.

The earliest account is that of St. Paul (I Cor. 15: 3–8):

> For I delivered to you as of first importance what I also received, that Christ died for our sins in accordance with the scriptures, that he was buried, that he was raised on the third day in accordance with the scriptures, and that he appeared to Cephas, then to the twelve. Then he appeared to more than five hundred brethren at one time, most of whom are still alive, although some have fallen asleep. Then he appeared to James, then to all the apostles. Last of all, as to one untimely born, he appeared also to me.

The Synoptics and John credit Mary Magdalene with the first vision of the risen Christ, which, even had it occurred, would probably not been thought worthy of mention by St. Paul, who had a low opinion of women. In any case the knowledge of the Resurrection, except for Christ's general appearance to the five hundred, was regarded as the peculiar privilege of the Palestinian disciples. But Mark, whose opinion of this group seems none too high, perhaps did not even mention the Resurrection appearances to them.

Whatever had happened it was clear to the apostles that Christ was risen, the greatest of miracles. This was an attribute of divinity, one which would be hard to deny if one accepted it. Furthermore, they believed that Christ would return shortly—how soon was not clear—that he, indeed, had told them that he would return soon. If his message had been merely one of great urgency, that Christians could and should produce a kingdom of heaven on earth, it was easy to believe that the heaven would be produced miraculously by a returning Christ. It is evident from Acts that the earliest Christians, at least at Jerusalem, did believe this, awaited the coming of the Lord, and were only slowly disillusioned by his failure to appear in the form expected.

Paul, as can be seen from the quotation, already had the vision of Christ sacrificed for the sins of the world. A world steeped in Isaiah would see in Christ's death the fate of Jehovah's servant (53:3—23 *passim.*):

> He was despised and rejected of men; a man of sorrows and acquainted with grief: and as one from whom men hide their face he was despised; and we esteemed him not.
>
> Surely he hath borne our griefs and carried our sorrows; yet we did esteem him stricken, smitten of God and afflicted. But he was wounded for our transgressions, he was bruised for our iniquities; the chastisement of our peace was on

him and with his stripes we are healed. All
we like sheep have gone astray ... And they
made his grave with the wicked and with a rich
man in his death ... (He) was numbered among
the transgressors: yet he bare the sins of many
and made intercession for his transgressors.

One wonders if the initial identification had been that of
someone who noticed the parallel between Joseph of
Arimathea and the "grave with a rich man in his death,"
for while Mark and Luke speak of Joseph as a man of respect, Matthew says that he was rich, a fact obviously
deduced from his having a tomb of stone.

The early history of the Christians from the Resurrection to the fall of Jerusalem in A.D. 70 is very obscure. It
was a period of forty years, a period which should have
been kept well in the memory of many. Most of us can
think back to 1926 and, by comparison, understand what
might have happened in the period. Of course they did
not have the ready communications of today. Thus, much
of the communication must have been distorted as the
message moved from person to person. Just how great
the distortion was, can in part be judged by the development of the life of Christ in the period.

X

The Possibility of Extrasensory Perception

In these days, when extrasensory perception is wide-ly accepted as a factor in human life,[1] the possibility of its appearance has to be considered in the life of Christ, and especially in the Resurrection. It is such an unusual and even awe-inspiring faculty that possession of it may give the person an outstanding reputation for superior and supernatural wisdom, so much so that it might cause him to gain a position of leadership by its use. The question might be raised as to its influence in lives like those of Mohammed, Joan of Arc, and Hitler, for whose careers normal explanations hardly suffice. So we take up the evi-dence which might seem to indicate that Jesus did have such power, evidence that he had experienced clairvoy-ance and precognition both about himself and about the Jews, Jerusalem, and the Temple. With this in mind one may consider his apparent walking on water, the Trans-figuration, and the Crucifixion as possible instances of ESP. It would be one interpretation of what happened, obviously different from the orthodox theory of bodily resurrection and appearance.

At the outset it would seem that Jesus had a reputa-tion for clairvoyance. "And some began to spit on him and to cover his face, and to strike him, saying, "Prophesy" (Mk. 14:65). It is made clearer in Luke (23:64): "They also blindfolded him and asked him, 'Prophesy! Who is it that struck you?' " Unless this was a standard humiliation meted out to those with a reputation for religious leadership, this would show a special attribute of clairvoyance to him.

There are several cases recorded which allege clairvoyance, two of them about persons who were supposed to be dead or dying. The son of an official at Capernaum was said to be dying, but the father was told, "Your son will live" (Jn. 4:50), and later found that his son had begun to get better at precisely the hour Jesus said that he would recover. In the second, Jesus told a crowd as he entered the home of the ruler of the synagogue, "Why do you make a tumult and weep? The child is not dead but sleeping" (Mk. 5:39). In either case it would have been a better story if he had been alleged to raise the child as if from the dead. Two stories of raising from the dead are given, so that this interpretation of what happened might quite well have been given (Widow's son, Lk. 7:14; Lazarus, Jn. 11:38—44). Another possible case of clairvoyance is that of Jesus' suggesting to Peter, James, and John that they should cast their nets again after a fruitless night, and their catching a netful of fish (Lk. 5:1—11). In all cases, of course, another interpretation is that Christ was the agent of the change rather than merely a clairvoyant participant at the scene. But one instance which is clearly not of this character was his statement that those who would arrest him were coming (Mk. 14:41—42).

Precognition is attributed to Jesus more than is any other type of extrasensory perception. Of the buildings of the Temple at Jerusalem, he said, "You see all these, do you not? I say to you, there will not be left here one stone upon another, that will not be thrown down" (Mk.

13:2; Mt. 24:2; Lk. 21:6). There is also the prediction for the city of Jerusalem (Lk. 19:41–44):

> And when he drew near the city he wept over it, saying, "Would that even today you knew the things that make for peace! But now they are hid from your eyes. For the days shall come upon you, when your enemies will cast up a bank about you and surround you, and hem you in on every side, and dash you to the ground, you and your children with you; because you did not know the time of your visitation.

The disciples were told of the sufferings which would come to them in the apocalyptic chapter (Mk. 13):

> For they will deliver you up to councils; and you will be beaten in synagogues; and you will stand before governors and kings for my sake, to bear testimony before them.

In several passages Jesus mentions his own fate. The statement in Mark (10:33) that he would be delivered up to the chief priests and scribes, who would condemn him to death and deliver him to the Gentiles, seems hardly in accord with possibilities. The anointment of his body for burial by a woman mentions only death, not a specific crucifixion (Mk. 14:3–6). The prophecy that the disciples would fall away (Mk. 14:27) again is precognizant.

Another instance of precognition is that of the appearance of Jesus to Saul (Acts 9:4–6; 22; 6–16) on the Damascus Road. Paul always felt that this was equivalent to the appearance to the disciples shortly after the Crucifixion and equally valid. Furthermore, other supernatural appearances were not attributed to Jesus even at the time. In Damascus it was the "Lord" rather than Jesus who instructed Ananias to see Saul and explain the situation to him. Earlier it was an "angel of the Lord" who opened the prison gates for the disciples (Acts 5:19 —20). A vision appeared to Paul as he was in a trance, declaring to him that all men were saved by Jesus (Acts 5—10). Thus there was no indiscriminate attribution to the Spirit or to Jesus himself of appearances in the period. We should face the probability of another instance of extrasensory perception.

Three cases are given in which Jesus may have appeared in an incorporeal form to his disciples. The first case is that of walking on the water (Mk. 6:47—52; Jn. 6:19—21). "But when they saw him walking on the sea they thought it was a ghost." Now Matthew (14:28—33) embellishes the story by having Peter try also to walk on the water and be saved by Jesus extending him his hand. As a result, it is said, they recognized him as son of God, but, one wonders, if this had been true, why there was any doubt later. The second case was that of the Transfiguration (Mk. 9:2—10). Again, after the appearance of Jesus in garments "glistening white, as no fuller could bleach them," a voice came out of the cloud, after Jesus had conversed with Moses and Elijah: "This is my beloved Son: listen to him." The third was, of course, after the Resurrection, when Christ appeared several times to his disciples. Upon all three occasions the sonship of Jesus was stated in the Scriptures. These appearances were of the kind that might be associated with ESP.

Now ESP, it has been observed, is apt to be associated with crises rather then than with routine situations.[2] A woman calls to warn her daughter hundreds of miles away and saves her from danger. Or those who have just died appear to those who love or are interested in them.

It can be seen that most of the cases mentioned fall in the class of crisis situations. The disciples are fearful when they enter Jerusalem before the Transfiguration, or they seem in danger from high waves on the sea, or they have just suffered the trauma of the Crucifixion. Christ sees those believed dead and assures grief-stricken parents that their children live. Or in the hours before the Crucifixion, Christ has visions of the future of Jerusalem, the Temple, and his disciples. ESP then occurs in what seem to be its most natural circumstances.

In every case there are other possible explanations depending largely upon the basic ideas of the reader. Some of the statements seem so clearly to be myths to a class of readers that they find it difficult to accept statements as other than myths. Others trust implicitly in the written word and feel that only a literal interpretation of the writing need be accepted. In between one pursues a difficult course: whether to believe in an ESP interpretation, or some other rational and natural explanation of what is written. The original evidence has gone through many hands. May one assume that association with Christ has preserved the integrity of the evidence, or can one believe that even such evidence must have been reshaped in the light of theological beliefs and the appearance of myths about Jesus?

It leaves the believer or non-believer in roughly this position. The believer feels that he must accept either the written word or the interpretation of his religious organization. The non-believer finds that the believer is guilty of treason to human integrity. In between one must trust to a sense of historical-mindedness and to the satisfaction of honest adherence to a search for truth.

XI

Beth Peter and Beth Paul

According to the Gospels, Jesus appeared to about
five hundred persons in the course of the forty days
following the Crucifixion (I Cor. 15:3-9; Acts 1:3), sometimes in or near Jerusalem and sometimes in Galilee.
At the end of the period the apostles gathered in Jerusalem
to select a replacement for Judas Iscariot and to wait for
the Second Coming. However, of the apostles only Peter
and John are mentioned as remaining active at Jerusalem
(Gal. 2:9). The activities of the others constitute a major
mystery. Ancient and medieval writers assigned them as
missionaries in far countries, a sure indication that they
did not know much about them. The Jews then were
divided into groups of widely differing beliefs, so that
the addition of another group, the followers of Jesus,
provided no real novelty, and they were not noticed much
in the writings of the Jewish authors of the time. At
Jerusalem, then, there was a very sharp controversy between the followers of the former religious thinker Hillel,
(Beth Hillel) and of another, Shammai (Beth Shammai),
over the nature of Jewish faith and action. In beliefs of a
moral and spiritual kind (except for the nature of Jesus)
the Beth Hillel, in the person of Gamaliel, was probably
closer to the beliefs of Jesus than it was to the Beth
Shammai. Even among the Christians differences of belief might be expected.

At Jerusalem the followers of Jesus seem before long to have lost whatever organization there had been of an apostolate of twelve. Peter, whose original leadership was evident, spent much time in his missionary activities, being claimed eventually as the first bishop of Antioch and Rome. James, the brother of Jesus, soon appeared as the head of the Christian community at Jerusalem. The position thus approximated the hereditary high priesthood or head of synagogue of the Jews. Although the Christians preached in the Temple area, a very large place devoted to much besides the more strictly religious portion, they were probably associated also with the synagogues of the city. Normally a racial or geographical group would associate with a particular synagogue, presumably because they formed a little colony about it. One would have anticipated that the Christians, as primarily Galileans, would have worshiped in a synagogue at least partially composed of their fellow provincials.

However, at Jerusalem there was a definitely Hellenist group among the Christians. Stephen, it may be recalled, disputed with "some of those who belonged to the synagogue of the Freedmen (as it was called), and of the Cyrenians, and of the Alexandrians, and of those from Cilicia and Asia" (Acts 6:9-10). One suspects that it was a Hellenist group with which Stephen argued, perhaps even in the synagogue where Christians normally met. And the rift between the Galileans and Hellenists may have had its origins in the fact that the two groups attended different synagogues and thus seemed to belong to different social groups, each of which should have cared for its own indigent (Acts 6:1–6).

It is clear that there were differences of belief among the followers of Jesus at Jerusalem. The problem there, as elsewhere, was essentially a question of whether Jesus

100

as the Savior (about which all agreed) was just another, if very great, prophet or whether he was more closely related to divinity. A Jewish prophet had a very high place: he listened to and spoke with God; he might be a great political leader, such as Moses; and he would certainly be a great moral leader of the nation. Some of these, by a liberal interpretation, were almost divine qualifications. Even the term "Son of God," if parallel to the expression "Our Father in Heaven," might be accepted for a Jewish prophet. Yet there was a limit to this relationship. Where did the religious power end and magic begin? And with this question went also the question of whether the beliefs of Jesus implied an acceptance as well of most of the beliefs and laws of Judaism. More definitely, should the Hellenists, particularly the uncircumcised, be required to adopt Jewish practices as a part of their belief in Jesus? Were they to be Jews as well as Christians?

Some have emphasized the importance of the great churches in the early history of Christianity, particularly in defining the canon of the New Testament. Yet the early Christian leaders were largely migratory and thus carried their ideas with them among the colonies of Christians. At Jerusalem as well as elsewhere, the differences of belief were evident. As Paul wrote, "What I mean is that each of you says, 'I belong to Paul' or 'I belong to Apollos' or 'I belong to Cephas' or 'I belong to Christ'" (I Cor. 1:12) and belonging often meant believing as the founder believed. Paul was interested, as many others were, in maintaining a fundamental harmony among the divergent points of view. Thus the differing interests in certain "gospels" may represent actual preferences in the congregations which accepted them. The constant migration makes it unlikely that isolation of a community prevented the use of say, Mark, in some areas of Christianity. Usually in a church one point of view would have sufficient majority to force the acceptance of particular books by the whole group.

At Jerusalem the pro-Jewish party was definitely in charge, even influencing Peter when he was there (Gal. 2:1-21), although he had at one time gone there to remonstrate with the "circumcision party." The close relationship at times between Jews and Christians kept them close in belief and, after all, Jesus had observed most of the Jewish practices. As we have seen, there was a party of Peter at Corinth, and the party of Apollos may have been more in favor of Jewish practices.

Another center of the pro-Jewish party was probably Capernaum. The existence of a Christian group there is made clear by Jewish writers of the time who told of the minim, the Christian heretics, there. While Jesus apparently felt that he had not been accepted well at Capernaum, his followers may have become important in the old synagogue and perhaps even took over after the Resurrection. Remains of an old synagogue have been uncovered, as well as those of a fine synagogue of about the second century A.D. Some of the apostles returned to the area immediately after the Crucifixion, and probably several eventually settled there into the life which they had known before. Not missionary-minded, they were probably content to remember the words and actions of Jesus and to enjoy memories of his life with them in the district. Furthermore, the site of Jesus' activities would before long have become the center of pilgrimage, and the men who had been his companions could tell of what they remembered. Capernaum would have been a notable source of information about his life and works. Such pressure on the local group might well have led to a recording of his sayings. The writings which have come down to us have, for the most part, come from the more strictly missionary centers and might well leave Capernaum and the neighboring towns without record during the missionary period. It can be assumed that Capernaum's point of view would have been local rather than ecumenical in character and thus more Jewish than Hellenist.

Jerusalem and Capernaum were on the interior line of communication through Palestine. Continuations of the line would extend, in the north, to Damascus and eventually to Antioch and, in the south, to Egypt and Alexandria. Both Antioch and Alexandria were great commercial cities and would be subjected to streams of Mediterranean influence. Despite this there was a party of Peter at Corinth, as has been mentioned, and probably also at Rome. We assume that in spite of his Gentile leanings at times, Peter was more favorable to a continuation of Jewish practices and points of view than Paul was.

The career of Mark, as far as it can be worked out from the meagre evidence, shows again the difference between the two points of view. His mother's house was apparently a Christian center in Jerusalem (Acts. 12:12). Yet he went with Barnabas and Paul to Antioch (Acts 12:25) and proceeded to Perga in Asia Minor on a missionary trip (Acts 13:5). But there he turned and went back to Jerusalem after apparently falling out with Paul. Papias, an early Christian writer, later asserted that Mark acted as an interpreter for Peter at Rome and wrote Peter's memoirs, that is, the Gospel of Mark. Mark, then, was apparently happier with Peter than with Paul for it was natural for a native of Jerusalem to prefer a Galilean to a Cilician and thus belonged to the Palestinian tradition. The Alexandrian community considered him their earliest leader, which is not surprising, since Alexandria

103

was on a continuance of the Capernaum-Jerusalem axis on the land route. Furthermore, Alexandria seems not to have shared in the initial missionary efforts, and thus may have become a center only after the death of Peter.

Both Alexandria and Cyrene, to the west, had extensive and powerful Jewish colonies in this period, so strong, indeed, that they experienced dangerous resurrections in the second century. Under these circumstances the Jewish groups were not apt to tolerate movements in their midst which did not largely conform to Jewish practices and which seemed only divisions of the Jewish community. Generally the Romans permitted the racial settlements within the large cities to control themselves and felt little urge to protect minorities within those settlements. This would be particularly true of the Christians in the early days if the Jews refused to accept them.

In contrast with the "circumcision" party, there was the Hellenist group, whose great leader was eventually Paul. But before his conversion, there was a Hellenist group at Jerusalem, even at the time of the Crucifixion. Where had it originated? Jesus' connections with such a group was possible only during his stay at Jerusalem, or possibly in Samaria during the course of his Mission. This raises again the question of whether Jesus had a considerable following of Hellenists outside of Galilee before the Mission. The rapid takeover by this group at the expense of the more strictly Jewish party can hardly be explained otherwise.

As a Hellenist center Caesarea played an obviously important part, as is clear in Acts. There Philip lived during his missionary work among the Samaritans. Paul and his fellow workers stayed there voluntarily and involuntarily for long periods during which they can be traced and probably at other times when they cannot be followed. As capital of the Roman government of Palestine, it must have shared in the Hellenism so typical of such government sites. A Christian movement developed almost spontaneously following the Crucifixion. The apostles at Jerusalem learned of it and sent Peter and John to it (Acts 8:14-24). It was already the nucleus of a considerable movement before Philip went to it as a missionary (Acts 8:4-8). From there Philip and doubtless others moved on to wider missionary efforts, particularly in Asia Minor.

The Church at Antioch seems to have been founded by missionaries from the Hellenist party. The persecution of Stephen was alleged to have sent men as far as Phoenicia, Cyprus, and Antioch (Acts 11:19). But probably even earlier Christians from Cyprus and Cyrene went to Antioch and spoke to the Greeks, as well as to the Jews. "News of this came to the church in Jerusalem and they sent Barnabas to Antioch." Barnabas was happy with the group, and went on to Tarsus, from which he brought Paul to Antioch, where they stayed for a whole year. Evidently the men of Cyprus and Cyrene were not sent originally from Jerusalem, for that group seemed rather surprised to hear of the Antioch development. And it is interesting that the followers of Jesus were first called Christians in Antioch. That is, the group apparently believed that they were not primarily Jews. As seen earlier, the custom of naming groups directly after a founder, that is, Christians, rather than followers of Christ, was an Epicurean habit.

In the first generation of such a movement as Christianity, the center for missionary effort and of education in beliefs normally would stay largely in the original homeland. In the case of Christianity this would be Palestine, with Capernaum, Jerusalem, and Caesarea as centers, and these would have great influence at the time. Only in a second generation would sites farther away, such as Ephesus, Corinth, and Rome, have become so important and have attained such leaders that they could influence the cult markedly. One is justified, then, in seeking sources of beliefs and points of view in the home sites first. Outside of Palestine difficulties sometimes multiplied, as with the pagan followers of Diana at Ephesus, who felt that the new cult endangered economic values of their cult (Acts 19:24-41). The missionaries had the same problems with the Jews abroad that they had in Palestine. Paul and Peter endeavored to maintain harmony and an identity of objectives in their work. Much of their work was apparently in the Jewish synagogues, where they tried to prove Jesus was the promised Messiah. Even there the questioning of the Jews must have shown the divisions of viewpoint among the Christians themselves, providing one of the problems which the leaders had to solve.

At first, apparently, the apostles thought that the crowning manifestation of Jesus' greatness, the Resurrection, following his career of miracles and preaching, should be sufficient to convince the Jews of his position as Savior. As Peter is alleged to have said, "Men of Israel, hear these words: Jesus of Nazareth, a man attested to you by God with mighty works and wonders and signs which God did through him in your midst, as you yourselves know—this Jesus, delivered up according to the definite plan and foreknowledge of God, you crucified and killed by the hands of lawless men" (Acts 2:22-23). One may doubt the statement of foreknowledge at that time. After all, the Acts were written much later. One of the great Christian controversies has been over the extent of this foreknowledge of Jesus. With the Jews the great problem was whether Jesus was, in fact, the Redeemer

foretold by Scripture. Crucifixion was too humiliating for
the Redeemer to have suffered, and they doubted the
Resurrection.

The arguments in favor of accepting Jesus as the
Redeemer and Savior centered on several points. The
first was, of course, that the Christians were Jews and
thus part of the Jewish tradition. This was the basis of
Stephen's discourse (Acts 7:1–53): the Christians were
even better Jews than the Jewish religious leaders. It is
the message of Paul (Acts 13:16–41) and also of Peter in
his several speeches. This was done primarily by asserting
that the career of Jesus was prophesied in the Old Testament: its several parts were foreshadowed by verses in
the Scriptures. For the next several centuries argument
continued by showing how Scripture referred to the acts
and the status of Jesus. Gradually, as Christians separated
from the Jews, Jesus took on the character of a universal
Savior, but still he was prophesied for the world as well
as for the Jews: Isaiah was a great help here. But even as
a division within the Jewish world, the Christians had
developed certain rites of their own.

The early meetings of the Christians naturally developed a pattern. St. Paul gives a picture of it (I Cor.
14:26): "When you come together, each one has a hymn,
a lesson, a revelation, a tongue or an interpretation."
"Remember the words of the Lord Jesus, how he said"[1]
was apparently one form of quotation, according to Knox.
The early Christians were fond of quoting from Isaiah
and Daniel, Enoch and Sirach which gave little biographical material but much inspiration and apocalyptic material. Both the Jewish and Greek groups had traditions of
writing. The Greek side was more personal: letters were
included as well as philosophical-religious writings, such
as the directions of Epicurus to his friends and the life

itself of Epicurus. It would be surprising if the Christians, even while waiting for the Second Coming, did not reduce at least some of the sayings of Christ to writing.

In the above description of a religious service, there is little to which Jews might take exception, if Jesus was revered as a prophet and perhaps as a savior in the very religious sense. However, carrying the position of Jesus to that of a divine leader would certainly raise serious objection. Furthermore, in the period A.D. 30–70 the Beth Hillel came under increasing pressure from the more belligerent society of the Beth Shammai, perhaps as part of the growing nationalism" which ended in the great revolt at Jerusalem. Thus one can assume an increasingly critical attitude on the part of the Palestinian Jews and on the part of the Jews of the Diaspora toward the more Hellenist attitude of the Christians. The refusal of the Jews to accept the Christians precluded them from the protection which the Jews enjoyed as a received sect in the Empire. To lose this protection placed the Christians in danger of Roman persecution, as in the time of Nero, as atheists, since they did not believe in the gods. Losing the protection of Judaism, they also lost much of their respect and affection for it and its practices. This naturally led to an effort to convert the Romans and to an increased bitterness toward the Jews for outlawing them.

Once the Christians were rejected by the Jews, they found themselves in the pagan world, a world full of gods with their many attributes of divinity. And many of the gods had been human, as Euhemerus had explained to the satisfaction of the learned. Alexander the Great had been one of these: stories circulated about the occasion of his birth. His patron goddess had been so busy attending his birth that she could not protect her temple from burning down at the time. Even in the Old Testament (I Sam.

1:1-3;21), people expected stories of this kind to prove the divinity or the greatness of important persons. The heavenly hosts were thought to be very near humanity: angels, archangels, principalities, and others—all are there not merely in Revelation but among the pagans as well. And many thought that since the appearance of such beings should have happened, it actually did happen and that it was proper to declare that they had happened. As more and more pagans entered Christian groups, they brought with them their ideas and points of view. No religion can accept large numbers from another religion without being influenced by the ideas of the new members.

Christianity seems to have spread rapidly after the fall of Jerusalem and the year of the four Emperors (A.D. 68-69). The city's fall doubtless encouraged many wavering Jews to join the Christians, while the civil war must have driven many to think of the future life in Christian terms. Unfortunately there is very little information about the Christian movement at the time. However, the family of the Flavian Emperors (A.D. 69—96) seems to have had members who were interested in Christianity, which assumes either a very remarkable or a very accidental rise in Christian fortunes at the time. The powerful and the educated now were ready for conversion, but for this purpose more sophisticated and better-written accounts of Jesus would be helpful.

The believers in the teachings and the person of Jesus found themselves a part of the Jewish and the pagan world at the same time. It is hard to explain the strength of the Gentiles in the early Christian movement unless some preparation had been made by Jesus in the years preceding his Mission in Galilee in the form of groups of persons who had known his teachings and were prepared to believe that he was the Savior as the result of the Resurrection. The two backgrounds, Jewish and Gentile, naturally had profound effects upon the early course of Christianity. Christians had to convince the Jews that Jesus was the Savior foretold in Scripture. They had to convince the Gentiles that he was the Savior of mankind. In even the first century it proved easier to convince the Gentiles than the Jews. The great discussions were to shape the sect's beliefs and traditions, much as the great controversies of later centuries were to fix credal and conciliar statements. These early discussions were also to be reflected in the early writings.

XII

Logia, Letters, and Memoirs

"When you come, bring the coat which I left with Carpus at Troas, also the books and above all the parchments," an early Christian, apparently confused with Paul, wrote (II Tim. 4:13). This tells something of the literacy and interest in reading of the early Christian group. Indeed, as we have seen, the presence of a document-conscious apostle, the tax collector, Matthew, might incline one to hope that he would record the sayings of Jesus. There were conditions which were not conducive to the writing of a biography and which have complicated the study of the career and teaching of Jesus ever since. The first was the expectation of the Second Coming, which seemed to make the writing of a biography unnecessary, at least to the first and waiting generation. Even if a biography had been composed, the Hebrew tradition of writing a prophet's life would have limited the author closely to the message of the prophet and would have included only such incidental details as would fix the message in a simple geographical and biographical setting. Then the Savior was assumed to have had his career foretold in the Scriptures so that prophecies about it must have actually portrayed events in his life which had to be included. And Jesus as a great religious leader attracted to himself miracles and myths, as the great prophet is expected to do.

111

However, the actual words and acts of the prophet were so sacred that they should be remembered indelibly and treasured carefully by those who had seen and heard him. These were the chief crosscurrents which shaped the traditions about Jesus of Nazareth.

Early Christian tradition gave priority to Matthew, who, according to Papias (Eusebius Eccl. Hist. III, 9), "put together the oracles (*logia*) of the Lord in the Hebrew language and each one interpreted them as best they could." The *logia* ought to have been the sayings of Jesus. If the report was accurate, Matthew associated the words of Jesus with those of the great Hebrew prophets of the past and wrote them in Hebrew, as those of the prophets had been. If Aramaic is meant, the language of the area, its Semitic character may have misled the early writers: it was all Hebrew to them! This would have been natural if Matthew had returned and remained at Capernaum, perhaps even continuing in his work at the customs station there. The material which appears in the gospels of Matthew and Luke probably derives from the *logia*: since Matthew has more of that type of writing than Luke, he may have included more of the *logia* than did Luke. Capernaum would have been a natural center for the dissemination of information about Jesus, and Matthew, as a writer of records, had the habit of writing and collecting information. The early tradition seems quite reasonable. This material, which is common to both of the gospels, is usually called Q. In any case, the idea of writing down information about the words and acts of Jesus may have had its inception in Matthew's early collection.

The material in Q, as defined, now seems to be divided into two great blocks in Luke, the first occurring in chapters 3 to 7 and the second from 9:51 to 19:27.[1] The first part contains an account of the baptism of John, the

Temptations, the story of the centurion at Capernaum, and teachings of probably the early period of Jesus' ministry, since John is still alive at the end. The second part begins when Jesus had set his face to go to Jerusalem, and sent messengers to a village of Samaria (9:52). His appointment of the seventy appears different from the sending of the twelve earlier, and the woes to Chorazin, Bethsaida, and Capernaum (10:13–15) suggest that Jesus was permanently leaving that area. The rest is interspersed with data evidently coming from the mission in Samaria and Judea just before he went to Jerusalem the last time. It ends with the parable of the pounds (19:11–27), a parable of the necessity of being prepared for the second coming. The arrangement of the material in Matthew is very different from that in Luke, but the latter seems to have preserved the original order better, if his treatment of the Q material is like the way he arranged his excerpts from Mark.

With repect to the relationship of God to Christ, Q seems almost more primitive than Paul. It is stated as in the Lord's Prayer, "Our Father, who are in Heaven (Mt. 6:9) and in such a statement as "You may be sons of your Father" (Mt. 5:44), and usually Jesus is called the Son of Man. It must be remembered that the definition of Q is made difficult because both Matthew and Luke individually certainly left out parts which the other included, and thus more of it must actually be present than can be defined accurately. It clearly seems influenced by earlier Scripture:

With respect to the relationship of God to Christ, Q seems almost more primitive than Paul. It is stated as in the Lord's Prayer, "Our Father, who are in Heaven (Mt. 6:9) and in such statement as "You may be sons of your Father" (Mt. 5:44), and usually Jesus is called the Son of

Man. It must be remembered that the definition of Q is made difficult because both Matthew and Luke individually certainly left out parts which the other included, and thus more of it must actually be present than can be defined accurately. It clearly seems influenced by earlier Scripture:

> And in that day shall the deaf hear the words of the book, and the eyes of the blind shall see out of the obscurity and out of darkness. The meek also shall increase their joy in Jehovah, and the poor among men shall rejoice in the Holy One of Israel (Isa. 29:18–19).

> Go and tell John what you have seen and heard: the blind receive their sight, the lame walk, the lepers are cleansed, and the deaf hear, the dead are raised up, the poor have good news preached to them. And blessed is he who takes no offense with me (Mt. 11:4–6; Lk. 7:22–23).

> Behold, I send my messenger, and he shall prepare the way before me. (Mal. 3:1). What then did you go out to see? A prophet? Yes. I tell you, and more than a prophet. This is he of whom it is written, "Behold I send my messenger before thy face, who shall prepare the way before thee" (Mt. 11:9; Lk. 7:26).

The two early centers important for early Christianity outside of Galilee seem to have been Jerusalem and Caesarea. Of these the more aggressive was certainly Caesarea, with Paul as the outstanding missionary leader after the first decade or so. But almost from the first it probably was the chief Gentile center. Philip was the apostle of Samaria, presumably among the Gentiles as well as among the Jews. Caesarea was an obvious source of information about the mission and message of Christ since, Jesus had been in the area for some time. As a more aggressive area it needed more material, better written than oral, for use in the debates which any missionary effort required. Three sources of this early period seem to belong to the point of view of the Gentile-oriented Christians: the letters of Paul, the material in Luke (after chapter 2) which is not in Mark or Q, and possibly the information which appears in John, which, oddly enough, would seem to offer much information about Christians in Jerusalem in the time of Jesus. Probably later than Q, these data would seem to be the earliest surviving Christian information besides Q.

In a famous statement St. Paul declared that more than five hundred persons had been witnesses of Christ resurrected (I Cor. 15:3–9), "most of whom are still alive, though some have fallen asleep." Given the argument of Paul, one would expect the tendency to be toward exaggeration. If the estimate is correct, the time should not have been more than fifteen years after the Resurrection, using a life table prepared from the inscriptions of Asia, Greece, and Illyricum.[2] If there was actually an interval of twenty-five years, say from A.D. 30 to 55 or thereabouts, the surviving number of witnesses would be about 28.5 percent of those aged twenty or above at the time of the Resurrection, and about 30 percent of those aged fifteen years at that time. Perhaps it is too much for one to expect that Paul would have been an accurate observer in matters such as these. He might have not noticed the deaths of lesser persons, and thus might have underestimated the number of deaths of all Christians in the period.

St. Paul was much more interested in the death and resurrection of Christ than he was in his life. He men-

115

tioned that he saw the brother of the Lord, James (Gal. 1:19), that Christ was rich (II Cor. 8:9), that Christ was meek and gentle (II Cor. 10:1–2), and that on the night of the betrayal he broke bread and drank wine (I Cor. 11:23) "in remembrance of me for a new covenant." The very lack of information from Paul about the life of Jesus was a tremendous hindrance to the creation of a biography, for the letters of few others of that generation have survived. The very heavy emphasis upon the resurrection encouraged by Paul obscured an interest in Christ's life. Paul mentions little of the Christian message, although it may be conjectured from the information and advice in the letters. Nevertheless, Paul's emphasis upon celibacy, the subordination of women to men, and the synagogue rather than small groups as centers went beyond what Christ apparently taught. Even Paul was apparently influenced by Scriptural references to the "root of Jesse" and its application to the genealogy of Christ.

And further, Isaiah says (Rom. 15:12):
The root of Jesse shall come,
he who rises to rule the Gentiles;
in him shall the Gentiles hope.

The quotation from Isaiah (11:10) reads: "And it shall come to pass in that day that the root of Jesse, that standeth as an ensign of the peoples, unto him shall the nations seek; and his resting place shall be glorious." To St. Paul this apparently was a clinching argument that Jesus was of the line of David: the Letter to the Romans begins, "Paul, a servant of Jesus Christ ... who was descended from David according to the flesh and designated Son of God in power according to the Spirit of holiness by his resurrection from the dead, Jesus Christ our Lord." It is not surprising then that genealogies of Christ were presented by both Matthew and Luke as going through Joseph. And St. Paul, writing "God sent forth his Son, born of woman—that we might receive adoption as sons" (Gal. 4:5), gives the impression that Christ also was a son by adoption, the same line as the genealogies going through Joseph. And in John (1:45): "We have found him of whom Moses in the Law and also the prophets wrote, Jesus of Nazareth, the son of Joseph."

Although the letters of others besides those of Paul add to the knowledge of early Christian belief, they add almost nothing to the knowledge of the life of Jesus. In fact, the biography of Jesus must be written upon the information in the Gospels, evaluated by study of the sources themselves.

Did Paul also have with him a copy of the *logia?* If it was in Hebrew, he, as an educated Jew, could probably have read them. The content of a section of his epistles to the Romans (12:14–21) resembles sayings from the Beatitudes (Mt. 5:4–10; Lk. 6:20–38). However, the passages do not read like a direct quotation or even like a paraphrase made after reading them:

> Bless those who persecute you; bless and
> curse not them. Rejoice with those who rejoice,
> weep with those who weep. Live in harmony
> with one another; do not be haughty, but asso-
> ciate with the lowly; never be conceited.

These read like notes which one takes either while listening to the speaker or writes down afterward. On the other hand, the beatitudes are evidently more literary and are better arranged. What is evident is that the series of ideas were already together and in circulation. It seems likely, then, that Paul either had taken notes from the *logia* or had a copy of them with him. It is too long a se-

117

ries to be remembered casually. While there are many places where ideas which seem to be in common with Q appear, this is only natural, since many of the stories and ideas of Jesus would have been in circulation. However, Paul does not quote Christ (I Cor. 7:10; 9:14) in the same way as he does the Old Testament, and apparently did not think of Q, if he had it, as part of Scripture.

Like Matthew, the present gospel of Luke is a compilation. Indeed, it is very much like Matthew in that the first part is apparently later and the rest includes both Q and Mark. In addition, there is a body of material peculiar to itself which may be called L and which, since it also is early, should have come from Luke.[3] The data in L seem to have three special interests: women, Samaria, and governmental connections. One recalls the story of Mary and Martha (10:38–42), the only son of the widow (7:11–17), the blessing on Jesus' mother (11:27–28), the woman with an infirmity of spirit (13:10–17), the lost coin (15:8–10), the widow and the judge (18:1–8), and, of course, the statement about the women who were with Jesus in the mission. "And also some women who had been healed of evil spirits and infirmities: Mary called Magdalene from whom seven demons had gone out, and Joanna, the wife of Chuza, Herod's steward and Susanna and many others." Besides the story of the Good Samaritan there is the story of the thankful Samaritan among the ten lepers (17:16). The section begins with a very exact statement of the governors of the Tetrarchy (3:1–2), mentions Pontius Pilate and the Galileans (13:1–5), and has several references to Herod (9:7; 13:31; 24:10), the last the very unusual association of Herod and Pilate at the time of the crucifixion. All these suggest a woman interested in or close to government, and point to Joanna, the wife of Herod's steward, who doubtless lived at Tiberias, the seat

118

of Herod's government. References to Samaria would suggest much comes from Jesus' stay there. One wonders if some of the stories may not have been given by Jesus to groups of women: this might explain why they did not appear in the *logia* of Matthew, assuming that they were the collection known as Q.

If the source of much of this information was Joanna, Luke or some intermediary may have picked it up at Tiberias, assuming that she returned there sometime after the Crucifixion, during the years that Luke was in Caesarea and Paul was in prison. The interest of Luke, assuming that he wrote Acts also, continued in a series of references to Caesarea (8:5; 9:32,35; 10:1–48; 21:7,16; 23:34). Few miracles occur in this part of Luke: the healing of the eighteen years' infirmity and the raising of the widow's son. There are also but few attempts to assign to Jesus something forecast in earlier Scripture. Indeed, one always has to remember the possibility that an event actually occurred and that later someone assumed that a particular reference in Scripture foretold it. With this important qualification, the references in L which have some connection with Scripture are given.

Before the incidents of the final week, in few places does the influence of Scripture appear, except for the very general statement early in Luke (4:16):

> He opened the book, and found the place where it is written: "The Spirit of the Lord is upon me, Because he has anointed me to preach good news to the poor" (Isa. 61:1–2).

> He set his face to go to Jerusalem. And he sent messengers ahead of him, who went and entered a village of the Samaritans, to make ready for him; but the people would not receive him,

because his face was set toward Jerusalem. And when his disciples James and John saw it, they said, "Lord, do you want us to bid fire to come down from Heaven and consume thee and the turned and rebuked them (Lk. 9:51–55).

And Elijah answered and said to the captain of fifty, "If I be a man of God, let fire come down from Heaven and consume thee and the fifty. And there came down fire from heaven and consumed him and his fifty" (I Kings 1:9–16).

Elijah's revival of the son of the widow (I Kings 17:17) is much like the incident of the reviving the widow's son at Nain (Lk. 7:11–17). Elisha also was reported to have revived a child (II Kings 4:32–37).

The Gospel of John may have been written by John the Elder in Ephesus near the end of the first century from material which he secured in part from about Jerusalem.[4] Although the source did not know the country to the north of that city well, he seems to have had a close acquaintance with one or more of the apostles. The one usually selected as the source was John. However, references to John as the beloved apostle rather militate against this assumption, especially the downgrading of John in the list after the Resurrection (Jn. 21:2). Matthew almost certainly would not have reported on the order of apostles in that way. The stories told about Peter are not very flattering. A gay story about Nathaniel's reference to Nazareth is all that is mentioned about him, even if he is Bartholomew. The prominence, however, of Philip the Apostle is rather startling. He introduced Nathaniel to Jesus (1:44), discussed the problem of feeding the 5,000 with Jesus and Andrew (6:5), was requested by some Greeks to see Jesus, and then conferred with Andrew

120

(12:21), and later asked Jesus (14:8), "Show us the Father," a question which seems to have been on the minds of all. Philip was apparently not on the shore of the Lake of Galilee (21:2) when Jesus appeared to several apostles, and thus apparently did not go back to Galilee. The act of the Greeks in selecting Philip as intermediary suggests that Philip was known at Jerusalem and thus probably was the unnamed disciple who knew the high priest and went to him with Jesus (18:15–18), reporting upon Peter's cowardice at the time. Important men at Jerusalem, such as Nicodemus (3:1–15; 7:50–51; 19:39) and Joseph of Arimathea (19:38–42) figure heavily in the narrative. The story of the Samaritan woman in John (4:7–30; raises the possibility that it also may have come from Philip, the apostle to the Samaritans.

Now just at the point where Philip might have been expected to take his place among the prominent Christians he disappears and is alleged to have died later at Ephesus. At precisely this point Philip the Evangelist appears, having exactly the kind of career that one might have expected of Philip the Apostle. He is one of seven who are appointed to look after the interests of the Hellenists at Jerusalem (Acts 6:5); goes to Samaria where he had much success at a missionary, converting even the local magician, Simon, (8:4–24); reads the Scripture and explains it to the eunuch on the Gaza Road (8:26–39); preaches from Azotus to Caesarea (8:40); and eventually entertains Paul at Caesarea (21:8–9). As a personal item, it was recorded that he had four unmarried daughters who prophesied (21:9). He also is alleged to have died at Ephesus or in Asia Minor. The difficulty of identifying the two is that the seven who saw to the Hellenists' interests are assumed to be different from the apostles (6:4–6) and that the apostles remained at Jerusalem

(8:1), while Philip and others went to Samaria. It is also difficult to assume that Philip, if the apostle, would have followed Stephen in the list, even though Stephen was the first Christian martyr. Despite these objections, the similarity of the two careers and characters, their common resting place in Asia, and the ease with which one career would follow the other, make a good case for identification. Even if we assume that John the Elder got information from Philip or other apostles and disciples in Jerusalem, the exact information is hard to identify. Not many miracles appear in John, and two of those which do seem to come from Mark.

Thirty years after the death of Jesus the number of persons who had ever seen and heard him would have declined to less than a fourth (assuming them to have been at least fifteen years of age in A.D. 30). Shortly after A.D. 60 there occurred the martyrdom of Peter and Paul at Rome and of James at Jerusalem. Although many still awaited the Second Coming, its possibility retreated year by year, until the Gospel of John explained (what was accepted only gradually) that the Second Coming had occurred in the appearance of the Logos or Holy Spirit. Thus the message of the Mission and Resurrection depended more and more upon the authority of Jesus as he had lived and died on earth. Two types of the good news did appear in the next two generations. The first type, like the earlier L and Q, began with the baptism of John and continued to the Resurrection, but emphasized the biographical element more. To this type belonged Proto-Luke, Mark, and John. Later, when the divine character of Jesus came into question, Matthew and Luke were written. For the Gospels, like the later creeds, were produced in part to satisfy the theological problems which arose.

The author of Luke, perhaps Luke himself, explained that he was compiling a narrative or "declaration of those things most surely believed among us, just as they were delivered to us by those who from the beginning were eyewitnesses and ministers of the word" (Lk. 1:2), in answer to a request for such an account. This was in the preface of the final version of what is our present gospel of Luke, but doubtless the preceding version, Proto-Luke, was prepared under similar conditions. Since Hebrew tradition knew little of biographical writings, it was only natural that a group with strong Gentile background should have felt the need for such an account, which would fall in line with the biography so typical of the Greco-Roman culture of that day. It is likely, then, that the so-called Proto-Luke preceded the more purely Jewish work of Mark, and provided a precedent for the latter.

Proto-Luke was apparently produced by Luke about A.D. 60 by the joining of Q and L. Probably he acquired much of the information at Caesarea, during his stay there. The result which has been attributed to Luke begins with the present third chapter of Luke and continues to the end without the selections later added from Mark.[5] It thus begins with the baptism of John and the temptations and finishes with the Resurrection, but is very weak in the Galilean sections of the ministry. Presumably the author was the Luke who is spoken of as the "beloved physician" (Col. 4:14). His gospel does not seem to have more than the usual number of medical terms, but he did use the expression alleged by Jesus, "Doubtless you quote to me this proverb, 'Physician, heal yourself'" (Lk. 4:23), and he chose the Q version of the issue of blood, which left out the following: "and who had suffered much under many physicians, and had spent all that she had, and was not better but rather grew worse" (Mk. 5:25–26; Lk.

123

8:43–48). In any case, Proto-Luke was a gospel with relatively few miracles and with little recourse to Scriptural prophecy. It did include a genealogy of Jesus going back through David to Adam (3:23–38), which indicates that already the impact of Scripture had caused Jesus to be considered a member of the royal house.

Early Christian writers asserted that the Gospel of Mark was the memoirs of Peter and that it was written at Rome, where Mark had been an interpreter for Peter. From the gospel it would seem that it was dictated and that the person referred to most frequently is Peter. The center of the action is Galilee, and Jerusalem appears only at the end of the Mission. Mark was evidently from Jerusalem, and as has been suggested earlier, his point of view was more sympathetic to the pro-Jewish group than to the pro-Gentile. It would have been surprising, then, if Mark had not written in part to present a more congenial picture of the Mission to those at Jerusalem and Palestine than had been presented in L, which defines the biography of Jesus in Proto-Luke. That Mark was also thought to have been the original leader in Alexandria rather suggests a strong pro-Jewish group in that city. Peter is portrayed as a very human person in the Gospel of Mark. One gathers that, in spite of his impetuosity, Peter was a rather humble person who could delight in telling stories of his own failings. Even if he denied Jesus three times in the night before the Crucifixion, he was probably the only apostle close enough to have the chance to do it. Much of the confusion in the account of those last twenty-four hours resulted from the lack of accurate witness by the apostles.

Few evidences remain of the impact of Scriptural prophecy. Isaiah's story of the messenger is associated with John the Baptist rather than with Jesus (Isa. 42:1;

Mk. 1:1), and the story of Herodias may have been influenced by that of the Queen of Sheba (6:23; Esther 5:3, 6) about the importance of the half of the kingdom. The evidence of the growth of legend seems clearer, particularly at the end.

There is the story of Mary Magdalene, Mary, mother of James, and Salome going to the tomb and finding there the young man, dressed in a white robe who said, "Do not be amazed; you seek Jesus of Nazareth who was crucified. He is risen, he is not here; see the place where they laid him. But go, tell his disciples and Peter that he is going before you to Galilee; there you will see him as he told you" (Mk. 16:5–7). Now, Paul wrote nothing of this. The explanation for its lack of circulation (16:8) was "And they went out and fled from the tomb; for trembling and astonishment had come upon them; and they said nothing to anyone, for they were afraid." Then there is the problem of the Little Apocalypse (13) where, in contrast with other parts of Mark, some quotations from Danniel appear (7:13; 9:27; 11:31; 12:11).

Before Mark, indeed, there seem to have been related relatively few miracles on the part of Christ. Q mentioned them only in a general way (Lk. 7:21; 10:9) and L had two cases. St. Paul had only a dim opinion of miracle makers (I Cor. 12:28–29): "And God appointed in the church first apostles, second prophets, third teachers, then workers of miracles, then healers, administrators, speakers in various kinds of tongues." But with Mark there comes a steady flow of accounts of miracles in the Gospel: recoveries from fever (1:29), from many sicknesses (1:31), from leprosy (1:40), from paralysis (2:5), from a withered hand (3:1); calming the storm on the sea (4:35); curing the insanity of the Gerasene (5:2); raising the daughter of Jairus (5:35); stopping the flow of blood

(5:25); the feeding of the 5,000 (6:40); walking on the water (6:48); curing the daughter of the Syrophoenician woman (7:21), of deafness (7:32), of blindness (8:22); the Transfiguration (9:2); cure of dumbness (9:20), of blindness (10:49); annihilation of the fig tree (11:44). Mark may represent the new emphasis upon miracles in the West, since he is presumed to have written at Rome about A.D. 60–70.

The fourteenth and fifteenth chapters of Mark reflect many ideas from the Old Testament. The first come from a variety of places: the betrayal (Ps. 41:9), the blood of the covenant (Ex. 24:8), the desertion of the disciples (Zach. 13:7), and the "son of man sitting at the right hand of Power" (Dan. 7:13–14). The Crucifixion evoked references principally to the 22nd Psalm, the terrible psalm of lamentation: the casting of lots for the garment (22:18), the reviling of the crucified (22:7–8), and the concluding cry of despair (22:1). The offering of vinegar at the end has a parallel in the 69th Psalm (v. 22), which would seem a contradiction of the story in John in which he received wine and hyssop, seemingly a potion to cut the pain (19:28–30).

The Gospel of Mark is a most interestingly told account, and naturally was widely read; it was eventually included in the fuller gospels of Luke and Matthew. If it was written at Rome and appeared as the memoirs of Peter, it carried with it the prestige of the great apostle and of the chief religious center (after the destruction of Jerusalem) of the early Christians.

As the beginning of the Gospel of Mark shows, the author believed in the Sonship of Jesus, "The beginning of the gospel of Jesus Christ, the Son of God" (1:1). Christ is to come into the glory of God and his holy angels (8:38). The other references, and they are several (1:11; 3:12;

5:7; 8:29; 9:5; 12:35–37; 14:61; 15:39), are simple statements of the idea but do not explain the relationship any farther. The association of Christ in the Transfiguration with Moses and Elijah rather inclines one to believe that Mark still held to the theory of the adoption of Christ (9:5). If he wrote at Rome about A.D. 60–70, a most sensitive place, he tends to indicate that the question was so uncertain that he did not suggest adoption or actual sonship of God.

One problem in the development of a biography of Christ is the apparently rapid turn to a mythological cast after A.D. 70. The fall of Jerusalem was possibly one factor, in that there now grew up an even greater anti-Jewish feeling, in which Christians tended to share. One result might be for the Christians to emphasize their distinctness from the Jews and to place upon them more blame for the death of Christ while emphasizing such acts of kindness or consideration as the Romans had shown. A second factor was the crisis of the Empire itself. It had under the Julio-Claudian dynasty enjoyed a century of peace (31 B.C.– A.D. 69). Now both the peace and the Julio-Claudians had gone in a clash of conflicting armies. This must have given the world a rather terrible shock at the time: the century of peace had gone. What would follow? It was a good time for the apocalyptic writings, such as Revelation, to stress the fear for the future and to urge the abandonment of reason, faith in the empire, and refuge in a Savior who had suffered on earth. The increase in those who might be attracted to Christianity included a great many of the literate persons of the Empire. Indeed, it seems likely that at least one member of the imperial Flavian family was a Christian and suffered for it.

The failure of the Jews to react favorably toward Christianity—indeed, the second persecution before the

127

siege of Jerusalem, the murder of James, and the flight from the city—doubtless helped in developing an anti-Jewish attitude. The reduction of a purely Jewish attitude toward divinity in favor of a more Greek attitude may have resulted from the weakening of the group of leaders who adhered more strictly to Jewish practices and ideas. The increase of Greek influence would perhaps have had the effect of releasing a flood of stories centering about the birth and death of Christ, emphasizing his divinity. Another Greek custom, particularly among the more learned Greeks, was an interest in serious manuscript and textual study. This, along with a similar tendency of the Jews, would have led to an increased search in the Scriptures for references which might be considered pertinent to the career of Christ. The birth of Christ was thought to be of divine origin and foreshadowed by a number of texts.

The Gospel of Luke is essentially Proto-Luke, to which is added the material from much of Mark and also two chapters at the beginning, possibly from family memories of Mary and others. Perhaps Luke himself reworked the material, mostly by placing parts of his sources in blocks, with relatively little change in order within the blocks. On the other hand, "Matthew" is a thorough reworking of Mark and Q, with additional material like Q which may also have come from the *logia* attributed to Matthew. The question of whether there was an M, in the sense of a well-organized document from which "Matthew" drew materials not in other known sources, is highly debatable.[6] The author of Matthew so obviously revised his sources as he combined them that the changes may be the result of his editing rather than of a separate source. He doubtless used a scattering of traditions in the changes which he effected. The beatitude "Blessed are the poor" becomes "Blessed are the poor in spirit," which is very different in meaning although the words change little.

Matthew may have been the answer of the pro-Jewish group to the exposition by the pro-Gentile group in Luke: it seems to have been written later. But both were subject to some of the same influences, notably in the need to explain the birth of Jesus. This could be done through the stories which Mary or some of the family remembered about the trip which the family made at the time of the birth of Jesus and which may have lasted some years at Jerusalem. The very simple facts of what was evidently a great event in the life of the family were shaped by Scriptural connotations and legendizing until the opening chapters of Matthew and Luke developed into typical opening chapters of the life of a great prophet and hero.

Under the impact of these influences John, the son of Zechariah, became John the Baptist. Joseph became a descendant of David, only to be set aside by the Virgin Birth. The site of the birth was moved to Bethlehem, travelers giving small gifts become wise men from the East bringing treasures, shepherds coming in from the fields are told of the birth by an angel of the Lord, and Herod slaughters the innocents of Bethlehem instead of just his own sons. Simeon and Anna find in Jesus the Savior they were praying for in the Temple. Out of the simple story of a village family comes the well-heralded birth of the Jewish Savior. The difficulty is, of course, that if even a fraction of these things had happened, there would have been no need for a crucifixion and Resurrection: the signs would have made Jesus' mission clear before he was thirteen years old. If, indeed, anyone doubts such a construction on the basis that it could not have happened, a glance at the fantastic stories told of Jesus in the time immediately succeeding this period of the writing of the opening chapters of Matthew and Luke will make the possibility certain.

With these opening chapters the Gospels attained

their present form, with perhaps slight modifications in detail later. The public to which Matthew and Luke were addressed was a more sophisticated group than that for which Mark was written. Better Greek appears in the former, and in Matthew there is an extensive rearrangement designed for a more logical and readable form. Perhaps even a little later the Gospel of John, presumably by John the Elder, author of two of the letters of John, appeared to explain that the Second Coming was already achieved in the appearance of the Logos as a comforter and adviser of the faithful. That the early Church was willing to accept four such divergent accounts which not only differed in point of view but occasionally contradicted each other illustrates the power of faith in the Christian tradition coming in these divergent forms. It was a faith in Jesus above and beyond an adherence to the belief in the writings themselves.